MARY PU

Remembering
Matt Talbot

VERITAS

This edition published 1990 by
Veritas Publications
7-8 Lower Abbey Street
Dublin 1

First published 1954 by
M.H. Gill & Sons Ltd
Dublin

Copyright © Mary Purcell 1954, 1990

ISBN 1 85390 185 7

Cover design by Philip Melly
Typesetting by Printset & Design Ltd
Printed in the Republic of Ireland by
the Leinster Leader Ltd

Contents

Foreword	✠ Joseph Carroll	5
Author's foreword		7
Chapter 1	One of 'the Talbot crowd'	9
Chapter 2	The ne'er-do-well	20
Chapter 3	Damascus on the North Strand	30
Chapter 4	The hard climb back	43
Chapter 5	In Martin's timber yard	54
Chapter 6	Matt and his union on strike	67
Chapter 7	The Great Strike and after	79
Chapter 8	A poor man helps the poor	91
Chapter 9	Sick, suffering and unemployed	101
Chapter 10	Matt reaches his summit	112
Epilogue		125
Appendix 1		127
Appendix 2		129
Appendix 3		130
Appendix 4		132
Scripta		136
Bibliography		139

Foreword

When I was a young priest studying in Rome I had a friend, an Italian Monsignor, who was working in the Congregation for the Causes of Saints in the Vatican. We used meet regularly to 'swap' languages. I hoped to learn some Italian from him, and he was anxious to become fluent in English. I remember upbraiding him one day, all in good humour, of course, for the small number of Irish saints who had been canonised by the Holy See. This was at a time when the last Irish saint to be canonised was St Laurence O'Toole, seven hundred years before. He replied, with a twinkle in his eye: 'The reason is obvious. You don't need them. After all, every second person in Ireland is a saint'! Facetious though he may have been, he was making a valid point. God raises up saints for public veneration when there is need of them. In the prayer of the Mass for Holy Men and Women in the *Missal* we read: 'May their prayers and example encourage us to follow your Son more faithfully'.

Few will deny that we need a saint of the calibre of Matt Talbot in Ireland and elsewhere today.

For one thing, he was a layperson. And this is the age of the laity in the Church.

He was a working man — 'one who stands out as a beacon of light for Irish workers' (Stephen McGonagle, a President of the Irish Transport and General Workers Union).

He was, for many years, an alcoholic — and the most recent statistics for under-age and teenage drinking in Ireland have shaken us all. We are living in an age of self-indulgence. We need the example of an ascetic like Matt Talbot to restore some measure of self-discipline. His life of penance is well known and the details are fully dealt with here. They are not always understood. They are sometimes even misrepresented. One of the merits of this book is that it places these physical penances within the context of Irish spirituality. One of the distinguishing marks of the early Irish Church was its austerity. This austerity consisted largely, as St Paul puts it, in 'chastising one's body' by fasting and vigils and bodily punishment. This form of penance was practised by the early Irish monks to an unusual degree. Now Matt Talbot, I venture to say, was in this tradition. He was a sort of throwback to the early Irish monks. A glance at his reading material in the appendices of this book will indicate his interest in their lives. He did not practise these austerities for their own sake, no more than did the Irish monks. They were motivated by his recognition of the need for reparation for his own sins and the sins of the world. One last point. He is a model for us today in his devotion to the Mass and the Blessed Sacrament. A certain decline has set in, for various reasons, in our reverence for the Blessed Sacrament. We need the inspiration of his faith in the sacrament of love. There is some reason to believe that the cleanliness of his person, for which he was remarkable, was deliberately cultivated out of reverence for the Blessed Sacrament.

The distinguished author, Mary Purcell, is to be thanked for having given us this revision of her splendid book. It deserves to be widely read. One has only to read it to be convinced that the canonisation of the Venerable Matt Talbot would bring great grace to the Irish Church and to the Catholic Church throughout the world.

✠ Most Reverend Joseph A. Carroll
Titular Bishop of Quaestoriana

Author's foreword

This book, first published in 1954, has been re-issued more than once in its original form, later in a shortened edition and as a small pamphlet. During the intervening years further information on Matt Talbot has accumulated. People who did not give evidence at the Enquiries into his life initiated in 1931 and 1949 were located. Thanks to Fr Morgan Costelloe, Vice-Postulator of Matt's cause, and to the makers of film and video documentaries, interviews with many of these individuals were recorded.

In the present work this new material has been interwoven with what was already known. Several recent re-readings of the sworn evidence given at both Enquiries convinced me that some witnesses confused dates, relating incidents that took place at different periods of Matt's life as if they had occurred earlier or later. One witness is described in a marginal note as 'excitable and irrevelant; an unreliable witness'. Two others gave hearsay evidence, based on what the unreliable person told them.

Of the more than fifty witnesses I interviewed before and since 1954 those who most impressed me were the men who worked with Matt Talbot in T. & C. Martin's. The death of Paddy Laird, Cabra, in 1985 means that we have lost the last link with the workers who were closest to Matt. I felt privileged to have known and talked with them.

This new edition presents Matt's life as it progressed, year by year, from birth to death, against the backdrop of the changing fortunes of Dublin from the second half of the nineteenth century to the early days of the Free State. It seems fitting that one who could claim to be, like Paul of Tarsus 'a citizen of no mean city', should today be remembered anew and his life story re-told.

1

One of 'the Talbot crowd'

For Dubliners, Friday, 2 May 1856 was a holiday. Law courts and public offices remained closed; the shops were shut. A grand parade was on its way from the Phoenix Park through the city centre to Dublin Castle. It halted at designated points at each of which the Lord Lieutenant, the Earl of Carlisle, proclaimed the peace treaty concluded between her Majesty Queen Victoria and Alexander II, Tsar of all the Russias. The north quays and city streets were decked with bunting and Union Jacks. Titled ladies and officers' wives watched from high windows; all along the route citizens jostled one another to get a better view while barefoot urchins clung to railings and lamp posts.

His Excellency, resplendent in scarlet uniform with silver facings and epaulettes, rode his favourite bay. Seven militia regiments preceded him, the 3rd Dragoon Guards and the 16th Lancers formed his escort, infantry and artillery followed, with the Lord Mayor in the State Coach bringing up the rear. Roars of applause followed each reading of the proclamation. It was good to know that the Crimean War was over, but some wondered whether all who had gone to the Crimea would return in the transports sent to fetch them back to Dublin.

After the parade most people hurried home to get something to eat; later they would turn out again to see the fireworks display. On the North Strand they cheered the 2nd Cheshire militia returning at quick march to Aldborough Barracks. In a nearby house, 13 Aldborough Court, Charles Talbot's wife was visited by neighbouring women who commiserated with her for having missed all the excitement. Elizabeth Talbot had more pressing, more personal concerns to keep her at home. On that day her second son, the boy she would call Matthew, was born.

Charles Talbot and Elizabeth Bagnall were married in the church of St John the Baptist, Clontarf, on 19 September 1853. The priest who officiated entered the usual particulars in the parish register: the date; the names of the contracting parties and their witnesses, Thomas Mills and Anne Kelly; finally his own signature, Edward Kennedy, CC.

Few Clontarf villagers would have had the time to stand and stare as the couple emerged from the church. It was the busy season in the seaside village. September being the first of the months 'with an R', the oysters were in and work on the oyster-beds was already in full swing. September was also the time when the sea-water was at its best and bathers in their bathing boxes had to be towed out and back as the tide surged and ebbed. A visiting writer, Francis Gerard, in his work *Picturesque Dublin, Old and New*, dismissed Clontarf as 'drowsy, behind the times, rendered insupportable by the smell of rotting seaweed and the sight of its disreputable bathing boxes.' The Talbots hardly bothered to wait there but turned their steps citywards, where, in the words of a popular Dublin ballad, they enjoyed their post-wedding celebrations:

> With a whole afternoon
> For their honeymoon
> Down by the Liffey-side.

There were many sights to be seen in Dublin that day. The Rotunda Gardens displayed

> The Wonders of the Human Creation
> THE AZTEC LILLIPUTIANS
> A new race of people hitherto supposed
> to be fabulous or extinct. Unique,
> Strange, Beautiful Creatures.
> Music: The Aztec Polka
> Admission one shilling.

One of 'the Talbot crowd'

In the Phoenix Park Franconi's Imperial Circus, with real Sikhs, was staging the Battle of Gujarat. This show was timed to coincide with the Field Day of Her Majesty's forces, drawn from all the Dublin military barracks. On a Field Day the Park was no place for a Dublin man to take a stroll. Before you knew where you were the recruiting sergeants would wheedle or bully you into taking 'the Queen's shilling'. New husbands were as liable as any to be enlisted, so bridegrooms not willing to join the red-coats kept well away from the Circus in the Park.

One could saunter down Sackville Street, the city's main thoroughfare, where a magnetic-telegraph line was being laid, admire the display of dahlias on Carlisle Bridge and go on to Merrion Square to see the Great Industrial Exhibition. At the entrances notices warned visitors to beware of thieves. Bill Coffey and his Swell Mob had profited financially from the Exhibition. Dressed to kill, as befitted their title, they had seen the exhibits several times, always leaving richer than when they arrived.

Whether the Talbots visited any or all of these attractions is not known. It was usual for a couple who had only one day's leave from work for their wedding to do a round of the city sights on their brief honeymoon. Charles had a home for his wife, a room in a not too dilapidated tenement house, No. 2 Lower Rutland Street. His earnings were fifteen shillings a week, about 75p in present currency, and he was in fairly regular employment. Thirty years old at the time of his marriage, he was a very small man with a rather aggressive manner.

Elizabeth, more than ten years her husband's junior, was plain-looking. Her name is not in the Clontarf baptismal register nor in other north city baptismal registers of the 1830s. This suggests that she was married from her employer's home. Marriages, then as now, were usually celebrated in the parish where the bride resided prior to her wedding. Girls in domestic service worked hard, but so did their counterparts in other countries. On the whole, those in Irish households were treated kindly, in many cases as one of the family. If a suitor came courting, the employer, regarding him- or herself *in loco parentis*, would enquire into the young man's intentions and his means of earning a living before the banns were called.

Little did Elizabeth Talbot think when she settled down in Rutland Street in 1853 that within the next twenty years she would change her address no less than eleven times. From the time of her marriage to her death sixty years later she was to know eighteen different homes. Could she have foreseen those eighteen 'flittings', one almost every second year for the first twenty years of her married life, her heart might well have failed her on her wedding day. Fortunately the future was hidden from the girl who became 'little Talbot's wife'.

Lower Rutland Street was a street similar to many in the north-central sector of the city at that time. A few residents still clung desperately to the gentility that had been theirs when the well-to-do lived in mansions on that street. Names of Rutland Street householders in 1853 included Rintoul, Pasley, Hales, Stubbs, Acheson, Babington, Eykelbosch, d'Aubertin and Crabbe, surnames which had a rather alien air about them. Placards with the notice, *Building Ground*, were in place from No. 7 to No. 16, from No. 35 to No. 46 and at other intervals in both Lower and Upper Rutland Street. For over fifty years fashionable Dublin had been following the lead given by the Earl of Kildare in moving his town house from the north to the south of the Liffey; as a result many a fine Georgian residence was listed in the street directories first as 'a tenement', then as a building site.

Between 1854 and 1874 Mrs Talbot gave birth to twelve children, nine of whom survived. Some were baptised in the Pro-Cathedral, some in St Agatha's church, North William Street. The parents' addresses, recorded in the registers of these two churches, show their constant moving about from one drab lane or street to the next, from one crowded tenement house to another. Rutland Street,

Summerhill, Aldborough Court, Newcomen Court, Montgomery Street, Byrne's Lane, Love Lane and other places long since demolished saw the Talbot family come and go. Their worst dwelling was in Love Lane, Ballybough; they spent most of the 1870s there before moving to a cottage in Newcomen Avenue off the North Strand.

Matthew, the second child, was baptised by Fr James Mulligan in the Pro-Cathedral on 5 May 1856. The young priest, only five years ordained, made an understandable mistake when entering the baptism in the register. He gave the mother's maiden name as Mullock instead of Bagnall. It was a common error at baptisms in the Pro-Cathedral, the godmother, when questioned, giving her own name instead of the mother's. The Talbots had cousins named Mullock and a Mullock relative was probably godmother to Matthew. But the mistake could have been due to the fact that it had been an unusually upsetting week for the clergy in the Pro-Cathedral, one Administrator, Fr McCabe (later Archbishop and Cardinal) moving out to his new parish and Canon Pope relinquishing the parish he had been promoted to a few months previously, to return as Administrator to the church where he had been curate. Fr Mulligan, barely twenty-nine, died in June of a fever contracted when visiting the sick and poor of the city.

In Matt Talbot's childhood there was no dole, no pensions, no children's allowances, no welfare clinics, no social services. Even water, that basic necessity, was not available in houses in slum areas. Citizens of Rutland Street and similar districts had to fetch every drop they needed from public fountains and horse troughs. After the Crimean war Dublin, like other cities where the British Army had strong garrisons, began to suffer from the inevitable backwash of the conflict. Every troopship that steamed into Dublin Bay was crowded with maimed soldiers and disbanded militia men. Soon the camp followers who made a point of always returning home with victorious armies arrived in England. The authorities took one look at these foreigners from every country in Europe and promptly shipped them to Dublin. Most of them settled near big military barracks; the area around Aldborough Barracks, near where the Talbots lived, became a red-light district, a warren for thieves and criminals of all kinds, where overcrowding and squalor were commonplace.

Dublin's population in 1850 was a quarter of a million. The city proper covered an area of about 3,500 acres and was almost enclosed in the nine-mile-circuit formed by the North and South Circular Roads. Two schools in the centre of that area claim the privilege of having had Matt Talbot on their rolls.

His first school was St Lawrence O'Toole's Christian Brothers' School; he was admitted on 8 July 1864, his age being given as seven years, whereas it was really eight years and two months. His older brother John had been a pupil in the same school from 1863; their address was given as Newcomen Court and their father's occupation as 'a cooper'.

Beyond a report on Matt stating that he was, 'kept at home through necessity', little is known of his progress, if any, in St Lawrence O'Toole's CBS. In May 1867 John and Matt were both admitted to O'Connell's Schools, in North Richmond Street, also run by the Christian Brothers. Matt was in a 'special' class, one for poor boys not likely to attend regularly or for a long period. They were taught the rudiments of reading and writing, learned their prayers, were given religious instruction and prepared for the sacraments.

At that time numbers of proselytisers were very active in the poor areas of the city. The campaign against them was spearheaded by the then Archbishop of Dublin, Paul Cullen, who was made Cardinal in 1868. During Lent 1867 he issued a stern pastoral letter warning parents of the dangers to the faith of their children and advising them to enrol them in the 'poor schools' run — on next to nothing — by religious. Matt paid eightpence for his reading-book, known as the

Christian Brothers' Second Book. It had Bible lessons adapted for the young by no less a person than the prominent writer and Christian Brother, Gerald Griffin. Stories about St Patrick, St Vincent de Paul, St John of God and the martyr St Felicitas were interspersed with lessons on nature study and science. Ireland, England and Scotland got two pages each under the headings of history and geography; there were lessons on cleanliness and hygiene; period pieces with self-explanatory titles such as The Thoughtless Boy, The Honest Sweep, Generosity, How to be Satisfied, and Honesty, imparted the authentic Victorian accent. Some world geography was taught indirectly through lessons on tea, sugar, oranges and similar commodities. The first lesson Matt Talbot was asked to master was on The Presence of God.

Reading was taught at that time by memorising the alphabet and the lists of nouns, verbs and adjectives printed above each lesson in the reading text. The teacher read a sentence and the class repeated it; when an entire lesson was read and understood the class chanted it over and over. There was a short but grim lesson on coal, followed by one on a garden, the latter being as much outside young Talbot's experience as a coal-mine. There were also poems and ballads, which were regarded as a pleasant variation. The first poem Matt ever learned was a hymn to Our Lady:

> Mother of mercy! day by day
>   My love for thee grows more and more;
> Thy gifts are strewn upon my way,
>   Like sands upon the great sea-shore.
>   Like sands upon the great sea-shore.
>
> Though poverty and work and woe
>   The masters of my life may be,
> When times are worst, who does not know
>   Darkness is light with love of thee?
>   Darkness is light with love of thee.

Remembering Matt Talbot

As this was always a favourite hymn with the old Dublin confraternities, it would have been well-known to the families of the boys in the Brothers' school and the puny Matt Talbot could join in when they sang the hymn at May processions and on the feasts of Our Lady. Two men who remembered Matt in the Men's Sodality attached to St Francis Xavier church, the Jesuit church in Gardiner Street, said that he had a very pleasant singing voice, 'but a big voice for his size. You wouldn't know where a man so small got so powerful a voice'. Pat Doyle was in his nineties when interviewed in 1952; he knew all the Talbot boys, some of them being his boon companions. He explained Matt's strong voice as inherited: 'He had a great shout, though he was such a bit of a man. And why wouldn't he? Sure the father had the very same shout; you'd hear oul' Charlie a mile away if one of the lads ruz his temper.' Young Brother Ryan, himself a fine singer, who had charge of this special class, must have looked with interest at the undersized boy with the outsize voice.

Alas, Matt's scholastic record was not brilliant. Two words served as his report for 1867, his first year at O'Connell's Schools: *A Mitcher*. For 1868 the brief report ran: *Kept at home through necessity*, a comment which had also been made in one of his reports from St Lawrence O'Toole's. That year the sum total of his attendance was three weeks, long enough to prepare for first Confession and Communion; in the following year he again spent three weeks in school and was prepared for Confirmation; but he considered himself a past pupil by then and was one of many boys who returned, unwillingly in most cases, to the evening religious class. His school career really ended in 1868 when he was twelve years old and eligible for work.

A twelve-year-old illiterate boy from Rutland Street was lucky to find work in the Dublin of 1868. Though business was brisk enough at the port, industry in Dublin and throughout Ireland had suffered a massive decline since the famine. Before that catastrophe the country had 696,000 workers in the textile and dyeing industries alone; by 1868 that number was reduced to 160,000. In the same period the building and manufacturing trades lost half a million workers, but general labourers, i.e. unskilled labourers, increased from some 30,000 to 130,000, and shirt-making ('that last refuge of destitute women', as Charles Booth called it in his work, *Ireland Industrial and Agricultural*, Dublin, 1901) employed nearly twice as many as formerly. The number of domestic servants also increased greatly. One had to eat to live, and work that promised regular meals was most popular in a country still in the shadow of the Great Hunger.

Matt Talbot got employment as a messenger-boy with the firm of E. and J. Burke at their stores in the North Lotts. The Burkes were wine merchants who also did bottling for Guinness's Brewery and for the Edinburgh brewers, Youngers. They had offices on the quays, at 16 Bachelors' Walk, and at 59 Abbey Street; their stores were in five different buildings in the North Lotts, the lane running between Abbey Street and Bachelors' Walk. He spent four years there and earned about four or five shillings a week, but in his next job he got six shillings a week, which was considered a fair wage for a boy messenger. The secretary employed by Burkes in 1953 remembered a very old employee who knew Matt Talbot from 1868 to 1872 'and could not say much to his credit concerning his time in our bottling stores'.

By 1868 Matt's father, Charles, was in charge of one of the whiskey stores at the Custom House docks. His wages had by then risen to a much-needed eighteen shillings a week. Besides John and Matt there were five younger children — Mary, Charles, Philip, Joseph and Elizabeth. To make ends meet Mrs Talbot went out charring. She and her husband probably considered themselves lucky, the average weekly wage being eight-and-six for men, four-and-eleven for women, and three-and-nine for anyone under twenty-one.

In 1867 the city was hit by a cholera epidemic similar to that of 1832. Dire poverty, bad housing and overcrowding all added to the appalling death-toll. In one year alone 5,000 people died of the disease. Archbishop Cullen, addressing the Poor Law Commission on what he had found in one Dublin workhouse, fulminated against the state of affairs there:

> Poor infants are brought to an untimely end. Corruption and profligacy have been promoted by the mixture of degradation and innocence. Family ties are broken. The old and infirm pine away in misery and suffering, in bitterness and affliction. Religion and charity have been banished. Poverty is not relieved but the poor are demoralised and destroyed.... And I would like to put any gentleman here on the diet given in the Union: two meals a day; a little oatmeal and milk each morning; bread and soup for dinner, and that every day in the year except Easter Sunday and Christmas Day, when ladies and gentlemen go to the workhouses to enjoy the sight, just as they might go to see wild beasts feeding.

Cullen, a Cardinal by 1868, was deeply concerned for the poor, especially the unlettered poor, who, he felt, were particularly susceptible to political agitators (one reason for his opposition to the Fenians), and to the hordes of alien proselytisers whose fanatic zeal to wean the Irish from their Papist superstitions was making inroads on his flock. As Matt Talbot went with messages from North Lotts to Abbey Street and Bachelors' Walk he would see the 'Soupers' singing their hymns and 'Songs of Truth'; ballad-singers, passing by, would jeer at them and retaliate with home-made ditties, like the satire about one Mrs McGrane who had gone up in the world but down in her fellow-Catholics' estimation:

One of 'the Talbot crowd'

> Ah, Mrs McGrath, did you hear the news?
>   But of course, me jewel, you knew it;
> The Quality's goin' to save our souls
>   An' pay us for lettin' them do it.
> There's Mrs McGrane, when her man was slain
>   On the banks of the bold Crimea,
> Gave her clergy up for the bit an' the sup,
>   An' took to Luther's idea.

Groups of children, with more zeal than manners, would surround a street-preacher or handbill man trying to distribute anti-Catholic tracts; they made sure to keep a safe distance while singing in shrill voices:

> Souper, Souper, ring yer bell,
> Souper, Souper, go to hell!

However, Matt Talbot could not always loiter when sent on messages. His elders and betters in the offices and stores would ask what delayed him. Besides, he might miss a chance of enjoying something 'not to his credit'. In the bottling store he found it easy to help himself to a pint of porter whenever he felt like it; there were evenings when he arrived home drunk. By the time he was sixteen his father, in charge of the bonded stores at the Custom House docks, got Matt a job as a messenger-boy there. John, then eighteen, had not mitched from school and, having mastered the 'three Rs', was already moving up to a responsible position in the Port & Docks Board. The boys were the third generation of Talbots employed there, their grandfather Robert being on the pay-roll as well as their father. As for Matt — if, while at Burkes, he had come home drunk from a surfeit of Guinness or Youngers, he now began to come home drunk on whiskey.

2

The ne'er-do-well

By 1870 the Talbots had moved to No. 5 Love Lane, Ballybough, a worse tenement than any of their previous homes. One boy, Charles, had died in childhood. Between 1871 and 1874 Patrick, Susan and a second Charles were born. At the time of Charles' birth, John, Matt, Bob and probably Joe and Mary were working, but the family was poorer than ever, most of the earnings being spent on drink.

Decades later Matt's sisters told how their father was very strict and thrashed Matt when he found out that the boy was drinking at Burkes; he arranged to have him taken on as a boy messenger in his own place of employment so that he could keep an eye on him. In 1952 I had several interviews with old Pat Doyle, a contemporary and neighbour of the Talbot brothers; he was also their 'drinking buddy'. Though then in his nineties Pat was quite lucid and convincing. He described Charles Talbot, senior, as a heavy drinker. Another elderly man, Tommy Ward, for years clerk of St Agatha's church, confirmed Pat Doyle's description of Talbot senior; both men completely disagreed with the evidence of Matt's sisters. Doyle thought highly of Mrs Talbot:

> She was a very hard-working woman. She had to be with such a houseful of them. Often she went out charring. She had her hands full with the lot of them but she could manage them, even Phil. He was known as 'the Man, Talbot,' he was about my age or younger. Terrible wild he was, even as a chap, roarin' 'I'm the Man, Talbot,' when he had the drop in. All of them had the liking for drink from their father. John, the oldest, would never touch it; he was the best of them,

steady like the mother. He was a great scholar, too; readin' and writin' and figures no bother to him.

The Talbots were terrible impudent when they had drink in. It was easy for them to get it on account of working in the Bonded Stores. They used have a can of whiskey in a bag sometimes. Matt's father had a powerful voice; you'd hear him shouting out the men's names; for a while he had a livery and a tall hat; but after some time John got that. (The Port & Docks Board records show that John was an official messenger wearing a uniform from 1870 onwards.)

Tommy Ward remembered playing Hunt-the-Cap, a favourite game of small boys in the Dublin of his boyhood, with the younger Talbot lads. He stated that Matt's father was often drunk on Saturdays, 'and very quarrelsome, too, when he had drink in'. As for Phil, who was seldom seen sober, 'He'd come rollin' up the North Strand, shouting, "I'm the Man, Talbot", and roarin' songs.'

Pat Doyle's reminiscences of the Talbots and their neighbours in the 1870s and early 1880s throw light on life in the North Strand area. He is worth quoting verbatim:

> One time the Talbots lived in a house with a garden; you could see it from the Canal. There was a quarry opposite the Ivy Church on the North Strand, a quarry filled with rubbish. Old grannies and children were picking cinders there; the children picked cinders for fires at home; the grannies looked for empty bottles, to sell them for the price of a drink. Drink was cheap then, tuppence a pint for porter and whiskey thruppence ha'penny a glass. If you brought in a sack of empty bottles to Fletchers, a drink and provision shop, they'd give you half a gallon of porter in a can, and the loan of the can an' a couple of tumblers. Publicans nowadays wouldn't trust you like that.
>
> There used to be a shebeen in Maggie Kavanagh's

of Great Britain Street (now Parnell Street); that was a good place for the crowd coming with the bottles, too. Maggie was well able to drink herself. She had barrels of brine with pigs' cheeks in them. Matt Talbot and the Man and myself often went there. When we had no luck with the bottles or no way of raising money for a drink we used steal a pig's cheek and sell it, God forgive us, and come back and buy drink from Maggie with the money we got for what we stole from her. When we'd plan a raid on the brine barrel, some would keep Maggie talking, the rest would stand in front of the fellow edging back to the barrel; he'd slip the pig's cheek under his coat and duck out.

A queer thing... Matt would never steal a pig's cheek; he always got out of it when his turn came; but he wouldn't refuse the drink when the fellow who did the stealing and the selling came back with the money. Matt was a coward in that and some other ways. When all of us would go in swimming above Annesley bridge on hot days he would never go in. Too fearful. We'd call him a coward. Maybe he wasn't but we called him one. I often stole pigs' cheeks from Maggie, God forgive me. I remember I had a navy blue coat and from having the brine off the pig's cheek dripping away on my coat, and the coat buttoned up against my chest, all the dye ran out of the coat. My poor mother said to me, 'That's a strange thing, Pat, after I paying four shillings for that coat at the Daisy Market.'

Ah, the Daisy Market! That's where our clothes were bought. The gentry's gentlemen used to sell their uniforms the minute they got a little worn, sometimes a coat mightn't have a *breac* on it. One Saturday night I got a trousers for one and eightpence, a dresscoat for tenpence — that was a powerful bargain! — and a brown bowler hat for fourpence. At that time Matt and myself were working for a Mr Poole who was building a skittle-alley out at Clontarf. The skittles were banished when the nuns came; too near the convent, you see. Mr Poole was a bit lame, but he was well-connected. When I went out that Monday with all my new clothes on me, Mr Poole takes one look at me and says he to me, 'Is it to a ball or building you're goin', Pat Doyle?' I got the sack on the spot. I must have been lookin' a bit of a masher all right, with my swallow-tail coat and my brown derby hat. But there were no unions in them days. You could be sacked for nothing.

John Talbot never came with Matt and me, stealing or drinking; but Bob would be there. He was a grand chap, and wild like Phil. Joe was the only big fellow in the family; they were all terribly small like the father. Sometimes we'd go to Rosie Plunkett's. Rosie was a washerwoman and Matt and myself would give her a hand turning the mangle. She did the washing for the soldiers in Aldborough Barracks. There was full and plenty in that barracks because all the Quarter-Masters were billeted there. Often they gave away pigs' cheeks for nothing; not out of charity but because they ordered too much and for fear the high-up officers would be coming inspecting. Old grannies with sons in the army used go up for free pigs' heads. Rosie, on account of having so much washing to do, used get as many as she could carry home, along with her pay for the washing, you understand. She'd sell them for far less than they'd be in the shops. She'd give Matt and me a pig's head or pig's cheek each for turning the mangle. She was a decent woman, Rosie. Then we'd sell it and go on a batter.

Times are changed. There used be wrestling matches in Fren's Gardens, near Ballybough Road. And in summer evenings and on Sundays young fellows would play Common (sic), hurling they call it now; our coats would do for goal-posts; we'd place stones on them to keep them steady. Outside the College on Clonliffe Road, too, we'd have games; Matt would never come, even to look on. Some of the lads would twist the ropes for the girls to skip. The Reverend gentlemen in the College were a bit down on that and there would be queer running if any of them came out.

Matt's father, Charlie, was a shocking man when he had the drop in; he'd kick the shins from under you and roar and shout something terrible. Young Charlie had a stand near Amiens Street (Connolly) Station and polished shoes for people in the street; he didn't live long. Bob wasn't very long married when he died. The Man — Phil — and myself went to his wake on a Sunday evening. I remember it well. Phil, the wildest of them all, was very small; 'twas he was the impudent fellow.

But I was telling you about Matt. He was a good hodman, everyone had to give him the palm for that. When he worked for Pembertons the builders, he'd do more in half an hour than the rest would do in an hour. The Master Builder or the foreman used to put Matt in front to make the rest of the men keep up with him. Mary Talbot married a slater named Andrews, Susan a baker, Fylan; Lizzie wasn't so young when she got married to a man named Courtney.

There was another shebeen — no licence, you know — at Hunters off Love Lane. We went drinking there. I'll say this for Matt, I never heard him cursing or swearing. He'd go to Mass but was in no way religious at that time. He only wanted one thing — the drink, never bothered with parties or dancing or card-playing. But he'd do any mortal thing for drink — think nothing of walking all the way to Baldoyle to hold horses for an evening. He often held horses for hours outside Carolan's pub on Howth Road and came home with a gallon of porter; we'd all help him to drink it. Everyone drank in those days, even the children had to get their half-gill. Ah, it's changed times.

The ne'er-do-well

In 1856, the year of Matt Talbot's birth, Fr Theobald Mathew, the Apostle of Temperance, died and with him the life of his great crusade. His magnetic personality and his powerful preaching evoked tremendous enthusiasm, but the vitality of the revival he inaugurated depended mainly on the man himself. His biographer, the Rev. Dr P. Rogers, wrote:

> Within a decade of the Founder's death the movement appeared moribund.... Of the five million Irish people who had taken the pledge only some one hundred thousand remained faithful.

In the 1860s over 1,500 licensed premises and almost as many unlicensed shebeens were doing good business with Dublin's population of a quarter of a million. Arrests for drunkenness during 1865 numbered 16,192, one-third of those arrested being women. Each year saw the number of deaths from intoxication rise; in 1862 there were four, by 1866 the number had risen to nineteen. Among the customs that spread throughout the city was an accepted system by which workmen were paid on Saturdays in the public-house nearest their place of work. They were paid in cash or had their pay-cheques or pay-orders cashed by the publican. Naturally, the latter took it for granted that, in return for his financial services, the men would spend some of their earnings on his premises.

A niece of Matt Talbot heard her grandmother, Matt's mother, tell of how Matt would come home on Saturday evenings, hand his mother a shilling, all that remained of his wages, and say, 'Here, mother, is that any good to you?' And Mrs Talbot, a patient woman, would reply, 'God forgive you, Matt! Is that the way to treat your mother?' Once Matt and his brothers stole a fiddle from a street musician, sold it and bought drink with the proceeds. More than once he came home without even a shilling for his mother; he would patter in barefoot, having pawned his boots to pay for his addiction. He attended Mass but during the early 1880s showed no further interest in religion. His family — aggressive, rowdy and quarrelsome — was not, except for the mother, the girls and John, a very exemplary one; their home was no haven of peace. Charles Talbot was made under-foreman at the Port & Docks Bonded Stores in 1882 and his pay rose to a guinea (twenty-one shillings) a week. A few months later he was pensioned off at six-and-eight a week, a sum which was increased to ten shillings in 1884.

Matt left the Port & Docks Stores in 1882 when his father retired and worked as a hodman for Pemberton's, the building contractors; he remained with that firm for some years, gaining the reputation of being a good worker. Although a man of small build, the drive and pugnacity of the Talbot blood spurred him on to prove that he was as good a worker as the biggest and brawniest man on the job. As Pat Doyle related, foremen got wise to this and put him first on the line of hodmen 'to set the pace.' He seems to have worked for alternate periods at Pembertons and at the Port & Docks, but whenever he was back with the latter firm it was as a docker, not at the Bonded Stores. Some supervisor must have noted that Charles and Matt Talbot were very partial to 'spirituous liquors'. John Talbot, however, was kept on and was promoted.

On one of the few occasions in later life when Matt referred to his earlier days he said: 'I should be the last person to advise anyone about religion. When I was young I was very careless about religion because of drink; and I broke my mother's heart.'

From his early teens until his late twenties Matt Talbot's life followed the same pattern, working hard and drinking heavily. He and his friends kept to their own area, that now known to voters and politicians as Dublin North Central; they were well known to publicans and shebeen-owners in Summerhill, the North Strand and Dorset Street. Mullett's, a public-house at the corner of Dorset Street and

Little (now Temple) Street, was much frequented by men of nationalist opinions and the Mulletts, James and Joseph, were on Police Superintendent John Mallon's list of those suspected of being members of Fenian or other secret societies.

Life in Dublin continued as usual. Horse-trams were introduced in 1874. In the same year St Agatha's parish, where the Talbots then lived, lost its parish priest, Fr Doran. While boating with friends in Dublin Bay, a squall overturned the boat and he was drowned; noted for his care for the orphans in North William Street convent, he was buried, as he had wished, in the orphanage grounds. The Earl of Spencer, Lord Lieutenant from 1868 to 1874, returned for a second term in 1882, his predecessor having resigned when Gladstone and Charles Stewart Parnell agreed on the 'Kilmainham Treaty', an agreement that seemed to promise a better future for Ireland. The Chief Secretary, 'Buckshot' Forster, also resigned; because of his coercion policy, attempts had been made to assassinate him; few regretted his departure from Dublin.

On 6 May 1882 Earl Spencer made his State entry as the Queen's Viceroy. With him was the new Chief Secretary, Lord Frederick Cavendish, second son of the Duke of Devonshire. Cavendish, married to a niece of Mrs Gladstone, accepted his new post with little enthusiasm and great apprehension. The Under-Secretary, Thomas Burke, held a permanent post, serving under successive Lords Lieutenant. He was an Irishman, a Catholic, a grand-nephew of Cardinal Wiseman; one of his brothers, Augustine Burke, RHA, was a distinguished artist.

Because Burke had served under Forster, the Invincibles, a secret society, decided to assassinate him on 6 May. Already that morning they had bungled an attempt on his life. In the evening the same men waited in the Phoenix Park, intent on killing 'the man in the grey suit', as one of the group identified him. Lord Cavendish chose to walk back alone from Dublin Castle to the Park. It was a lovely evening and many people were about. Soon after 7.00 p.m. Burke, who had taken a cab, was being driven through the Park when he saw his new superior striding ahead. He alighted and the two men walked along together. Further on they were surrounded and attacked by men armed with sharp knives. Burke died instantly. By the time a surgeon rushed up from nearby Steeven's hospital, the Chief Secretary was also dead. The killers escaped, some in a cab that went out the Chapelizod Gate, others in 'Skin-the-Goat' Fitzharris's cab through the main gate and down the North Circular Road. Black-bordered cards that read 'Executed by order of the Irish Invincibles' were left into newspaper offices.

Next day, Sunday, the city was in turmoil. Everyone knew of the Fenians but, up to then, the Invincibles had been unknown, unheard of. Leading Fenians in Ireland and America condemned the killing. Parnell, Dillon and Davitt, leaders of the nationalist party, did likewise. Homes of Fenians and known Fenian sympathisers were raided. Police were busy, troops were put on standby. In pubs men lowered their voices or looked over their shoulders before discussing the topic that engrossed every citizen. The regulars who drank in Mullett's pub, Dorset Street, were particularly wary. James Mullett, a Fenian, had been in prison since March, suspected of having murdered an informer, so he could not be accused of having had anything to do with the Park murders, but Mullett's was a meeting-place for men whose names were now being mentioned as suspects. Superintendent Mallon's men were noting who went in there; customers like the Talbots stayed away, looking for safer public-houses; an informer, a policeman or an Invincible might be listening to what a man 'with drink taken' might say. Pat Doyle remembered that fatal week well:

> On the morning after the Park murders there was terrible activity in the city; the police and the soldiers

were searching everywhere, our part of the city most of all. My father and myself and others, plenty others, had no wish to be questioned by them boyos. I'm not saying now that we had hand, act or part in what happened, nor even that we knew anything. But we had our own reasons for getting out, and getting a long bit away from Dublin that morning. So off we went, a crowd of us, down to Mayo, where we got work under the Congested Districts Board building Cleggan Pier.

I was never down in that part of the country before, and I found it very strange at first. Up to the day I left, Matt, Phil, Joe and myself used to be out drinking. 'Barney' was a nickname we had for Matt in Newcomen Avenue. I stayed down in the West for a long time, a couple of years, anyway. I got a bit lonesome down there, and after two or three years I came back.

It was a year of fear in Matt Talbot's area. An informer was shot dead in July near Amiens Street railway station. A man suspected of informing was stabbed in Hardwicke Street. Mallon, a Catholic and an Ulsterman, was tireless in pursuit of the men responsible for the Park murders. Some Invincibles managed to slip the net and escape to France or America; a few, the notorious Carey, his brother and three other Invincibles became Crown witnesses, their evidence convicting their companions. Five of those found guilty were hanged and eight condemned to penal servitude, 'Skin-the-Goat' Fitzharris and others getting life sentences, the remainder ten-year terms.

3

Damascus on the North Strand

A never-to-be-forgotten day in Matt Talbot's life took place two years after the Phoenix Park Murders, in the summer of 1884. For an entire week he stayed away from work and spent the time drinking heavily. By Saturday he was penniless, as was his brother Joe. Being 'on the slate' in local public houses they could not hope for further credit. They stood near O'Meara's pub on the North Strand, a strategic position on that day and at that hour. Dockers would be knocking off work for the weekly half-day and would come to the pub to draw, and drink, their pay. Among them would be friends whom the Talbots had often treated and Matt and Joe expected that the compliment would be returned now.

They were disappointed. For some reason not one man asked them 'if they had a mouth on them' — perhaps the two brothers had cadged drinks too often. Joe stayed on, still hoping. Matt turned on his heel and walked home. His mother, surprised to see him home so early and quite sober, was surprised when he looked for a clean shirt, tidied himself up and announced that he was going to Holy Cross College to take the pledge. Mrs Talbot was not impressed; she did not think Matt capable of keeping a pledge. 'Go, in God's name,' she said, 'but don't take it unless you are going to keep it.'

Holy Cross College, the diocesan seminary, stands on a wooded stretch of meadow flanking the Tolka river. Some historians hold that these meadows and a nearby wood, long since cut down, was the battlefield where the famous 'Battle of Clontarf' raged on Good Friday 1014 when Brian Boru broke the power of the Danes in Ireland. Hugo Doak, a Dublin poet of the present century, has commemorated

Tomar Wood, the Tolka, the battle and its aftermath in verse:

> In Tomar's Wood the axes rang,
> The red sap by the Tolka sprang,
> And many a towering warrior tree
> Bowed in its Easter agony....
> On field and shore the sun went down
> And on the walls of Dublin town,
> While from the stars a silence fell
> Upon the weeping citadel.
>
> River, that in a silver dream
> Mirrored the battle gloom and gleam,
> Within whose wave, whose passing wave,
> Died the bright image of the brave,
> Of all the wonder and the woe
> Forgetful now your waters flow,
> As if no woman ever sighed
> Or shed a tear at Easter-tide.

Cardinal Cullen built the College and the adjoining chapel; its crypt is his burial place. The property had once belonged to the man known as 'Buck' Jones, whose name was given to the present Jones's Road. Matt Talbot met a priest there, took a pledge for three months and went to confession. It has been stated that the pledge-giver was Dr Keane, one of the Seminary Professors, but Dr Keane left Holy Cross in 1883 and joined the Dominicans. Whoever the priest was he must have put Matt at his ease and spoken kindly to him. The penitent was still smarting from the snub received from the men who passed him by an hour before and was in the mood to respond to a kind word. He had been away from the sacraments for some years and was helped to make his peace with God.

On the following morning, Sunday, he received Holy

Communion at Mass. More surprises awaited his mother. On Monday Matt rose very early and went to 5.00 Mass in Gardiner Street church before going on to work at 6.00. He had no trouble finding work as his reputation for being a good worker was well-known. Builders and the Port & Docks Board had him regularly on their pay-rolls; he also worked as a temporary hand in T. & C. Martin's timber-yards.

Very little is known of Matt Talbot during the decade between 1884 and 1894. His mother told how he was sorely tempted to break his pledge, but when the three months were up he went back to Holy Cross and renewed it for six months and then renounced drink for life. His sisters noticed that he had a struggle to stop swearing; 'He used to have two pins stuck in the cuff of his coat to check himself when he felt like swearing.' He continued to go to 5.00 Mass daily and in the evenings, to avoid his former drinking companions, he went to a church and remained there praying until the church closed. Soon he was a familiar figure in Gardiner Street, Phibsboro and Berkeley Road churches. Matt's 'butties' were astounded at his changed ways, none more than Pat Doyle.

> When I came back from the West of Ireland I went around looking for the old pals, or for a fight — I was always fond of scrapping; one day I says to the lads, 'Where's Barney?' meaning Matt. 'Oh, Barney's a changed man,' they'd say and leave it at that. One evening I was in fine fettle, after a fight I had at the docks. I bet a big navvy twice my size. I was coming along the North Circular when someone says to me, 'There's Barney, Pat. Weren't you asking about him?'
>
> Sure enough there was Matt. *He* was looking for *me*, he said, so off we went together. 'So you're at it again,' he says to me. Wasn't that the queer salute after my years away? 'At what?' says I, lettin' on I didn't know what he was driving at. 'Fighting,' says Matt, 'Give

it up, Pat, give it up.' By then we were passing Fallon's pub and I asked him in for a drink, but he wouldn't come; he told me to go in, to have one whiskey and he'd wait for me.

I went in, got my drink and came out. I thought that maybe he owed money in Fallon's and was on the slate there. I forgot to ask him where we were going, but began to tell him about Cleggan and how we built the Safety Pier. I never noticed until he had me in the grounds of Clonliffe College. There was a Reverend gentleman walking up and down and reading his book. He seemed to know Matt well and Matt knew him.

'Here he is now, Father,' says Matt, 'I have him here to take the pledge;' and before I could say a word there I was on my knees taking the pledge. I was reaching for my hat that I had tossed on the grass when Matt says, 'Now that you have him here, Father, better get him to to go confession.' That was too much for me. I made a grab at the hat, missed it, jumped up and cleared off as fast as I could, leaving my hat where it was on the grass. Matt was very vexed with me for running away. I kept out of his way for a long time after that. The lads told me he didn't like how I ran from himself and the priest he seemed so friendly with.

Pat Doyle's story indicates that Matt and his *anam-chara*, the 'soul-friend' in Clonliffe, were by then well-acquainted. The late Dr Myles Ronan, replying to a query about who Matt's Clonliffe confessor might have been, wrote:

> He could have gone to a Fr McGrath, a Professor in the College in 1884 and the years that followed. Dr McGrath was the type of man who would be attracted by a character like Matt... Dr O'Donnell was Professor of Theology in Clonliffe at that time, he was also chaplain to Mountjoy Jail and kept in touch with all kinds of stragglers who called to him at the College

early and late. He would be the kind of man likely to take an interest in such a case as Matt's.

From 1882 to 1886 the College had as Professor of Philosophy, no less a priest than Fr Joseph Marmion, later to be known as Dom Columba Marmion, the great Benedictine Abbot whose spiritual writings have, in our century, been read worldwide. But there is no evidence that the paths of Matt Talbot and his fellow Dubliner ever crossed, though both lived in the same area of the city from early 1884 to late 1886. During that period Matt Talbot was on the first critical stage of his long spiritual odyssey, while Fr Marmion was deciding to leave his friends, his post in the College and his country, to 'seek God' in the way to which he felt drawn.

However there are some coincidences which indicate that Fr Marmion may have been the Clonliffe priest who befriended Matt. He was in the College from 1884 to 1886 and after 1886 Matt was often seen at the confessional of Fr James Walshe, SJ, who came to Gardiner Street that year and took charge of the men's sodality. Prior to Fr Marmion's appointment to Clonliffe College he had been a curate for almost two years in Dundrum; one of his duties there was to act as chaplain to the criminal lunatic asylum. In a letter to a fellow-student in Rome he wrote from Dundrum, 'I prefer hearing confessions to any other duty; great kindness and patience are necessary.'

The Fr Walshe to whom Matt turned for direction late in 1886 was a native of Ossory Diocese, but went to England and entered the Society of Jesus there on completing his studies in Carlow College. After his novitiate days he joined the Missouri Jesuit Province in America and spent almost two decades working in different cities in the States before returning to Ireland. By September 1886 he was in Gardiner Street. An obituary notice written at his death states that he was 'beloved by [sic] all classes, especially the working men.' Five hundred men of his sodality forfeited a half-day's pay to attend his funeral. His greatest memorial was the Penny Dinners for the poor — a boon in his area of the city. From 1892 to 1942, when the present Catholic Social Conference amalgamated a number of charitable works, Fr Walshe's Penny Dinners not only relieved the hungry and badly nourished but also preserved the dignity of those who came and who proudly told their neighbours 'I paid for me dinner.' The bills were another matter, but Fr Walshe was an able fund-raiser.

Matt's efforts to convert Pat Doyle to sobriety and a better life are typical of one but recently converted. He was not yet consolidated in virtue and had not learned to temper zeal with prudence, tact and patience. Lives of holy persons who experienced similar sudden conversions are full of such incidents. St Ignatius of Loyola, going on pilgrimage to Montserrat after his conversion, was overtaken by a Moor riding in the same direction. In the course of a conversation on religion the Moor made a reference to Our Lady that Ignatius considered blasphemous. He debated with himself as to whether he should stab the infidel or let him go. Finally he left the decision to his mount. At the next cross-roads he would drop the reins; if the Moor rode with him a dagger and maybe death awaited him; if he kept to the Camino Real, the Royal Highway, while Ignatius turned off towards Montserrat, he should go free. Luckily for the Moor, his mule rode ahead towards Barcelona while the burro carrying Ignatius plodded the road to Montserrat.

Undaunted by his failure with Pat Doyle, Matt tried to convert his brothers. Bob, who had married in the early 1880s died in 1886, but Phil, Joe and young Charlie were all still drinking heavily and had no intention of following Matt's example. In 1884 the Talbots lived at Newcomen Avenue; after 1886 they moved to Spencer Avenue. In 1890 Matt left home and took a room in Gloucester (now Sean MacDermott) Street. His married sister, Mrs Mary Andrews, lived nearby; she did the little cooking he needed and tidied his room. In 1937 she gave the following evidence regarding

Matt:

> For a long time after his conversion he was repaying money he owed for drink. He used to go into the public-houses where he got drink on credit and hand over the money he knew was due; then he would leave quickly.
>
> My mother told me that he and his brothers once stole a fiddle from a street player and sold it to buy drink. Afterwards Matt searched all the city and even went into all the poor-houses looking for the musician to repay him. But he was unable to find him.

The late John Robins of Clonliffe Road, a close friend of Matt since the 1890s, remembered how Matt tried to find the elusive fiddler. Finally he gave the money he had been holding for the man to a priest, asking for Masses to be said for the street musician's soul.

From time to time after 1890 Matt returned to his parents' home; in between these periods he lived alone. The records of the Franciscans in Merchants Quay show various addresses for Matt between 1890 and 1896. He joined the Third Order in 1890 when living in Gloucester Street, then he was with the family in Newcomen Avenue and again when they changed to Spencer Avenue; he lived alone in Upper Buckingham Street in 1895 and from 1896 until his father's death in 1899 he and his parents lived in Middle Gardiner Street. He could hardly have slept on planks between 1884 and 1890 when living with his family; he and his brothers would have had to share a room and probably beds, and it is unlikely that they would have agreed to share a plank bed and a wooden pillow.

Hardly anyone, not even his mother, realised what a complete conversion Matt's had been. Beyond the fact that he kept the pledge, repaid his debts, steered clear of his former 'drinking butties' and prayed constantly, his life to all appearances showed little trace of the tremendous interior renewal that had begun in 1884 and was steadily progressing. He was the same Matt Talbot, the same unskilled labourer, the same unimportant citizen of contemporary Dublin.

In one sense at least he had found permanent employment. To the service of God he brought the same verve and determination, the natural tenacity that had always distinguished him. Summing up his character, Pat Doyle said, 'Matt could never go easy, at anything.' The reserves of energy, the indomitable will that had hitherto dragged him down, now spurred him in a different direction.

His calling in life was a humble one, to fetch and carry for the trained men who specialised in certain trades and crafts. His daily work involved the carrying of bricks, mortar, heavy and hard-to-balance planks. A man bearing such loads walks with his head bowed, his eye continually on the ground; he is careful when mounting ladders, he takes the measure of passages through which he must manoeuvre unwieldy loads. Not for him to stand with foreman or architect, admiring this facade, watching that beam being swung into position. From the little we know of Matt Talbot during the first decade of his changed life there emerges a man intent on humbling and hiding himself, a worker attentive to his tasks, diligent and constant in all his occupations, spiritual and temporal.

Matt did not adopt the austerities associated with his name in the years immediately following his conversion. His friend John Robins told how Matt, to keep his mind off drink in the years after 1884, became a heavy smoker, smoking up to seven ounces of tobacco some weeks. 'When he decided to give that up he went to his confessor and took a pledge against it.' Paddy Laird recalled how his father, Bob, would bring Matt to their home when Paddy was a young lad and Matt would accept a cup of tea and whatever Mrs Laird offered with it.

Mrs Andrews and Mrs Fylan, sisters of Matt, giving

evidence in 1937, twelve years after their brother's death, stated under oath:

> After work until about ten o'clock Matt was hardly ever off his knees; he even ate his dinner on his knees. If someone called to visit he would sit down. At that time (1884-1894) he might take meat once or twice a week, or eggs for dinner. During Lent he took nothing only dry bread and cocoa, shell cocoa. Sometimes, but never on a Wednesday or a Friday, a little fish. He fasted from meat all June in honour of the Sacred Heart and the same for a week before big feastdays and the same in Advent. We seldom saw him at his prayers as he wanted to be alone. He would not eat any dainties, but on Christmas morning he would ask for a bit of tender steak to be fried for him. He usually lived on dry bread and shell cocoa without milk or sugar. One pound of sugar would last him six months.... He often referred to his past sins, saying, 'Where would I be only for God and his Blessed Mother?' He had a little statue of Our Lady and used to say, 'No one knows the good mother she has been to me.'

John Robins, Ted Fuller, Paddy Laird and other friends all described the constant and strong temptations to break his pledge during the first period when he took the three-month and then the six-month pledge. He himself told them of this. One evening he stood near a pub in Dorset Street, fingering the coins in his pocket, remembering the taste of porter, of whiskey. Finally he went in. None of the customers were men he knew and, though he waited a long time, no barman came to serve him; so he left, went to Gardiner Street church nearby and remained there praying until the church closed for the night. After that incident he never carried money on him again until late in life when he brought it to people in need or for charity collections. When Fr Cullen, a Jesuit, founded the Pioneer Association,

Matt Talbot was one of the first to join; his number on the register is 133.

It is interesting to note that when he sought compensation in smoking for his self-imposed sobriety, thus turning from one addiction to another, he got his confessor to administer a pledge against tobacco to him. His confessor at that time, according to his fellow sodality members, was Fr James Walshe, but he sometimes went to a Fr O'Callaghan in Berkeley Road and also to a Vincentian in Phibsboro. Fr O'Callaghan's brother, Ralph, a wine-merchant, was later to become Matt's friend. The Vincentian Father in Phibsboro has never been identified but could have been the saintly Fr Gowan, co-founder with Margaret Aylward of the Sisters of the Holy Faith. In *Reminiscences of a Maynooth Professor* the author recalls the impression Fr Gowan made on many students when 'he came to instruct us in the art of preaching and teaching Christian Doctrine.... we looked on that iron-grey, rough, plain man, not only with esteem but also with admiration and reverence. For if ever a man was in earnest, Fr Gowan was.'

Although we do not know who his regular confessor was from 1884 to 1896 we do know that early in that period Matt learned to read. For an illiterate man in his thirties it must have been a herculean task. Possibly his brother John, 'the only steady one of the Talbots and a great scholar,' according to Pat Doyle, helped him. Priests in Gardiner Street recalled a man who used hand a piece of paper through the grill after his confession and ask what a certain word was and what was its meaning; the man may or may not have been Matt Talbot. His heart must have failed him often in his struggles with the printed word and memories of days spent mitching from Brother Ryan's 'special class' for backward boys must have risen to reproach him. His experience in taking the pledge had helped; strength to stand firm was there for the asking as he found by praying when tempted to start drinking again. Similarly, when he encountered difficulties in reading he prayed for help, to the Holy Spirit, to Our Lady and the angels and saints. He told a fellow-worker who asked how he could possibly understand Newman's *Apologia pro Vita Sua* that 'when I get hold of a book like that I always pray to Our Blessed Lady and I believe that she always inspires me to take the correct meaning from the words.' When a foreman in T. & C. Martin's, Edward Carew, asked Matt what he was reading:

> He told me that he was reading the Book of Deuteronomy. I laughed at the idea and asked him how he could understand that. He said that he prayed to the Holy Spirit and so he would be sure to understand it. He did not say this in any spirit of ostentation.

In time Matt amassed quite a little library. From the leaflets and memorial cards etc., all bearing dates in the late 1880s and early 1890s, we can discover what he was reading at the period. It is evident that he was even then under the direction of some zealous and unusually perceptive priest, a priest who was himself a man of prayer.

First among the books he read at this and at all later periods of his life were the Scriptures. Because he was still only learning to read he went very slowly, so all that he read got time to sink in. He had several copies of the Bible, besides copies of the New Testament and a separate copy of St John's Gospel. He marked the fiftieth psalm, the *Miserere*, he had leaflets with this psalm, and he also marked two other penitential psalms and two chapters from the Book of Wisdom, Solomon's Prayer for Wisdom being on a well-thumbed page. Two of his collection of bibles seem to have been more used than others. One was covered with velvet, stitched clumsily over the original cover. The other was a pocket-sized New Testament which had evidently been carried about for a long time. The Passion of Christ is marked in each of the four Evangelists; St Matthew's Gospel was the most thumbed. Matt Talbot had been named for that other Matthew who 'rose up and followed' when the Lord called him at the customs-office.

The Sermon on the Mount is heavily scored, particularly the verses concerning anger and reconciliation, scandal-mongering and swearing and revenge, praying for enemies and persecutors, the need for prayer, fasting and alms-giving to be done solely to please God. The *Pater Noster* and several other verses in Matthew's Gospel got due attention. In St Paul the passage beginning 'Charity is patient, is kind' in Corinthians 1:12 was under-scored. Other books included one by the Benedictine writer Blosius and another by the Jesuit Rodriguez; Matt had a Franciscan Manual, and ten small volumes of St Augustine's *Confessions*, with a Life of St Augustine. Two books on the religious life raise the possibility that Matt may have considered entering a religious Order, or that his confessor advised him to read these books. Several lives of the saints, a book on prayer by St Teresa of Avila, church histories and catechisms were included in the little library — all second-hand books — that Matt bought, read and re-read during the decade following his conversion.

These books took the place of the men he used to drink with in earlier days. They trace the paths he took on the first stage of a long and arduous spiritual journey, the journey to God. The emphasis was on the need for constant self-denial, mortification and humility for a man whose goal was to be 'hidden with Christ in God'. One marked passage ran, 'In prayer man speaks to God; in spiritual reading God speaks to man.' Many of the books listed are now unobtainable except in religious libraries; they form our only link with Matt during the post-conversion years under review and are listed in Appendix I.

During this time, while the new Matt Talbot was gradually replacing the old, Dublin and Ireland were experiencing some exciting events. Echoes of the Park Murder Trials still lingered in the air. The memory of how Kilmainham Jail had been ringed round with ranks of Grenadier Guards, reinforced by infantry and police, while Marwood the hangman executed the Invincibles was still fresh in the minds of Dubliners. Pressmen showed their friends the cards he had handed to them, as was his custom; his cards were inscribed, 'William Marwood, Executioner, Horncastle'.

It was the decade of Parnell's rise and fall, with bitter recriminations between pro- and anti-Parnellites. One Irishman, however, paid little heed to the history being made all about him. For Matt Talbot the great events of those passing years were his victories over old habits, the conquest of discouragement because of his lack of education, the control of his temper. His joys were in learning: discovering the meaning of a word that baffled him, reading his ever-increasing hoard of books, copying in squiggly letters a text of scripture or a phrase that stirred some chord deep within his soul, like the words of King David (in Samuel 1:20,3):

There is but a step between me and death.

4

The hard climb back

The road Matt Talbot set out to travel in 1884 was a long and hard one, a road that was to stretch more than forty years into the future. He was the same Matt and had to accept himself as he was, with the same lingering wish for drink, the same Talbot temper with its short fuse; but he had, too, the same ability to work, to persevere with a task until it was finished.

Conversion, even the most dramatic, has its stages. In Matt's case, apart from turning away from drink and whatever sinfulness he acknowledged when he made a sincere confession in Clonliffe the day he took his first pledge, there was a slow but steady progress towards holiness. At a time when most men went to confession once or twice a year, he went weekly and to priests who were wise and experienced directors. They were men who advised him well, helped him to see and correct whatever stood between him and God, restraining him in the early years, encouraging him later to follow the inspirations received when the Lord invited him to 'Go up higher, friend,' on the paths of prayer and penance.

He did not succeed in governing his temper or his tongue for a long time and even in old age could speak sharply on occasion. Men who worked with him during the 1890s bear this out. Ted Fuller said:

> Matt was quiet but could be easily roused for a moment if things went wrong. He would then walk away in silence and 'cool down'. He would use harsh words on such occasions but never failed to ask pardon. I often heard him admit that he was wrong. When he discovered that he had been in the wrong he never

made excuses for himself but would say, 'You were right and I was wrong.'

Michael McGuirk stated:

> Matt had an abrupt way of speaking and could be blunt enough. He would always say what he thought. He was respectful to the managers but frank; he was not a 'boss's man'. He might get worked up arguing about something, but in a minute he'd come back and apologise.... We all thought highly of him; some might have a joke at his expense if they passed him at work — he was a great worker — but they were all fond of him.

Edward Carew, a foreman in T. & C. Martin's, attested:

> Matt was respectful to his employers but not servile. He was prepared to fight his corner if justice was at stake. He was strict with himself, but quiet, kind and gentle with others. Everybody was fond of him; he had no enemies. When Mr Murphy, foreman before my time, drew Matt's attention one day to a mistake in a list of planks given to a customer, Matt got a bit heated and said that it must have been the customer who made the mistake. He got quite 'ratty', but in a few minutes back he went to Mr Murphy and apologised, saying 'I'm sorry for speaking to you so crossly.' 'When Mr Murphy said, 'It's all right, Matty', he said, 'I'm sorry; I shouldn't have made excuses for myself.' Matt had an extraordinary influence over and power of handling men who were inclined to be bullies — an influence I could never exercise myself.

While waiting for the church doors to be opened before the 5.00 Mass in Gardiner Street, Matt would kneel on the

The hard climb back

steps, praying, if no one was around; but if others had gathered he would wait on the steps of the convent nearby, fearing that the conversation of those at the church door would impede his concentration on his prayer. On entering the church he would kneel and kiss the floor, then go to Our Lady's altar and light a candle before proceeding to his usual place, a pew from which he could see three altars. In those pre-Vatican II days Masses were offered simultaneously at different altars. He became annoyed if a certain Mrs L rushed past him to be first to light a candle; and he reproved another lady who used to lounge in an undignified manner in a pew, 'We must be reverent in the presence of the Blessed Sacrament and in the House of God', he said. One Ash Wednesday a fellow-worker commented on the dark, uninviting-looking brew — the milkless and sugarless cold shell-cocoa — Matt had for his midday meal. 'You know there's permission to take milk in tea and cocoa in Lent, now, Matt,' said the man, who was one of Matt's closest friends. 'Is that the kind of Catholic you are?' was Matt's disconcerting reply. These incidents happened during the years when Matt was struggling to control his naturally quick temper. Thirty years later, a leading Dublin medical man, Dr Moore, who treated him, could say that Matt was one of the gentlest men he had ever met.

In 1895 a new professor came to Clonliffe College. He was Dr Michael Hickey, fresh from his studies and ordination in Rome and he was appointed Professor of Philosophy by the then Archbishop, Dr Walsh. In the early 1890s Matt bought and read St Francis de Sales' classic, *Introduction to a Devout Life*. One chapter was devoted to the necessity of having a spiritual guide, 'no man being a judge in his own case, still less in his spiritual case'. Matt read that the one seeking advice needed humility, sincerity and confidence in his director, 'a confidence mingled with reverence, yet so that the reverence diminish not your confidence, nor your confidence hinder your reverence.' Francis de Sales, an outstanding director of saintly souls, summarised the virtues needed by the director: charity, knowledge and prudence. We do not know how Matt and Dr Hickey came to meet but in this priest Matt Talbot found a father and friend. Since he remained under Dr Hickey's constant direction for thirty years the question arises as to what kind of man Dr Hickey was. To have directed such a unique penitent, he must have been an extraordinarily enlightened confessor. The late Dr Myles Ronan, who had been a student of his and who later knew him as a priest-friend, gave the author his impressions of him:

> It is difficult to sum up his personality. He was the nearest approach to Pope(St) Pius X that I have ever met in my fifty-four years as a priest, and I knew both men well. Dr Hickey was a most saintly man and the most popular confessor imaginable — none of the students wanted anyone else. He was my own confessor for three years and his gentleness, advice and understanding were beyond anything I experienced in my time at Clonliffe. He inspired the College with a new spirit.
>
> He was one of the two chaplains the College supplied to Mountjoy Prison and was constantly receiving discharged prisoners.... Before they returned home they were, of course, hard-up for money and clothes but he never let them go without emptying his pockets. Often he must have seen through their stories and stratagems, but his kindness overlooked all that. He was a great-hearted man.
>
> He had not much of a singing voice but at clerical dinners and gatherings he had one party piece. It was a popular ditty that he picked up in Rome when a student at Propaganda College — a little Italian song poking fun at the Capuchin Fathers: *Padre Capuccino, siete un birbo!* (Capuchin Father, you are a rogue!)
>
> It was his rendering of this that used to give the

company such enjoyment. He'd stand there and sing it without any attempt at humour or interpretation.... No matter how often we heard it, his simple, childlike manner made it always sound fresh. He had been eight years in Propaganda and was a fluent Italian speaker.
His acts of charity were innumerable. I recall one in particular. There was a certain prominent Dublinman who had become a chronic alcoholic. The then Archbishop told Dr Hickey how sorry he was about this man. Immediately Dr Hickey went after the poor fellow, visited his almost daily, looked after him and was friend, companion and adviser to him until the end, when he was there to support him in his last moments.

Another Dublin priest who was one of Dr Hickey's students remembered him as 'learned, saintly and a professor we were all delighted to meet in and out of class. We loved him; sometimes he told us of a holy old Dublin man he often visited. In fact, we grew so accustomed to hearing him mention this character, that we regularly questioned him as follows, though we knew quite well what the answers would be:

'Where were you this evening, Doctor?'
'Visiting the old man I told you of.'
'You were a long time with him. What were you doing?'
'Oh, we sing hymns and pray for a while any time I visit him; then we chat. He's poor and lives alone; he's very holy.'

Besides his intellectual attainments and personal charm, Dr Hickey was undoubtedly a priest gifted with much discernment and wisdom. He had his reasons for allowing Matt Talbot to proceed from the lighter obligations he took upon himself in the years after his conversion to the severe bodily penance of his last thirty years. Throughout his life Dr Hickey retained an innocence and sense of wonder that neither time nor the contacts he made — with saints, sinners or cynics — lessened or marred.

It is obvious that he helped Matt's progress in reading. Apart altogether from the spiritual content of the books Matt read at the turn of the century, it is noticeable that he became increasingly capable of reading and appreciating books that made considerable demands on his memory and intelligence, books on controversial issues that required him to reason and arrive at conclusions. After 1900, events in Ireland had a tremendous significance for all Irish citizens; as will be seen this was reflected in the direction Matt Talbot's reading took.

For one thing, after 1895 Matt's reading covered a wider range. Apart from commentaries on the Scriptures, books on prayer and the spiritual life and lives of the Saints there were also historical works, doctrinal treatises and booklets and pamphlets on controversial subjects. An item which appeared to have been read and re-read was a reprint of a lecture given by Bishop Hedley entitled *On Reading*. Matt had the following passage heavily marked:

> Even when a newspaper is free from objection, it is easy to waste time over it. One may need to know of world events, but there is no need to absorb all the rumours, guesses and gossip, all the petty incidents in which the solid news is half drowned. This is bad for both brain and character.... Ideas, opinions, inferences and conclusions of every kind are presented, and the reader, taking in this prepared and digested matter, is deluded into thinking that he is exercising his mind. He is doing nothing of the kind. He is putting on another man's mental clothing, dressing himself in another's ideas... living the life of a child... talking second-hand talk.

The hard climb back

One wonders what the good doctor would have thought of the media a century after his time! An interesting point about Matt's bible-marks and marginal notes after 1896 is the passages he dwelt on. The psalms held a particular fascination for him, but whereas hitherto he had concentrated on the penitential psalms, especially the *Miserere*, now he moved on to psalms of gratitude and joy, e.g. Psalm 9:

> I will thank the Lord with my whole heart;
> I will tell of all thy wonderful deeds.
> I will be glad and exult in thee,
> I will sing to thy name, O Most High.

Psalm 29:

> I will praise you, Lord, you have rescued me
> and have not let my enemies rejoice over me.
> O Lord, you have raised my soul from the dead,
> restored to life those who sink into the grave.

Psalm 102:

> My soul, give thanks to the Lord,
> all my being bless his holy name.
> My soul, give thanks to the Lord
> and never forget all his blessings

Moreover, he underlined Psalm 31, which begins, 'Happy the man whose sin is forgiven.'

Some surprising books acquired at this period were a history of the Roman Empire, a biography of Peter the Great of Russia and a volume entitled, *Leo X and the Character of Lucretia Borgia*. This last may have been bought to help the reader argue with someone who was judging the Church and Renaissance Popes by the standards of the Borgias — ignoring St Francis Borgia who renounced his ducal title and great possessions in Spain to become a Jesuit. *University Life in the Middle Ages* and three of Newman's works indicate that his new director must have helped him with this ambitious reading programme. By this time Matt seems to have overcome his early difficulties in reading and was intent on accumulating stores of secular as well as spiritual knowledge.

Among his books were a profusion of leaflets, litanies of all kinds and membership certificates of confraternities and associations in Ireland and abroad. Most of these linked him to religious orders; the Franciscans, Dominicans, Jesuits, Carmelites, Augustinians, Vincentians, Redemptorists, Cistercians, Passionists and the Holy Ghost Fathers were among the Irish orders in whose confraternities he was enrolled and whose charities he helped.

Irish Catholics of the post-Emancipation period tended to copy the pious practices of English or continental Catholics. Cardinal Cullen, so long in the Irish College in Rome before his return to Ireland as a bishop, and his predecessor, Dr Murray, a prelate educated in Salamanca, encouraged this tendency. Yet we find Matt Talbot reverting to the spiritual ways of an older, holier Ireland. His austerities were reminiscent of those practised by the monks of Bangor, Skellig and Aran. His love of the psalms and litanies was in the Gaelic rather than the English or continental tradition. In early Christian Ireland the laity were attracted by the monasteries and flocked to join the monks in their devotions and liturgy. Many laymen were called Caogdach, or 'the Fifty-man' because they knew and could chant the three times fifty psalms. In 1899 Matt's father died, and Matt and his mother left Middle Gardiner Street for No. 18 Upper Rutland Street where Matt rented the basement. It was at this time that he added further penances to the severe fasting that had been his practice for more than a decade. His sister, Mrs Fylan, told how he slept:

> He slept on a broad plank the width of the bed, and he had a wooden block for a pillow. These he kept covered with a sheet and light blanket.... When I saw the plank and block first they were lying against the

The hard climb back

wall. When I asked him what they were for, all he said was, 'They're for a purpose.'

Again, some instinct drew him to imitate the austere streak that distinguished ancient Irish piety. The laborious lives of the early Irish monks was one aspect of the monastic life which was not so generally copied. While the gospel text about the lilies of the field that neither sew nor spin often finds favour, the same does not apply to the words of the master of the vineyard: 'Why stand you here all day idle?.... Go into my vineyard and work.' Matt Talbot, however, saw work as God's will, and his meagre pay as a means of helping those in need. He united work and prayer to a remarkable degree, which is no easy task. Prayer draws a person inward to that secret room, the soul, where God is waiting. Work draws one outward, towards other people and material things; close attention to the task in hand is needed if work is to be well done. Matt's way of overcoming the divergence between prayer and work was to remind himself of the presence of God. In one of his prayer-books he wrote in his strange script — for though he learned to read well, he never made much progress in handwriting — 'Everything I do is done under the eye of God.'

Matt Talbot's penitential practices scandalise some in an age when bodily ease and comfort have prior importance. Each day during Lent and again in June he observed a complete 'black fast', i.e. using no milk and taking only two light meals without meat or butter. Outside of these times his usual diet was: Mondays, dry bread and black tea or a tea-and-cocoa mixture; Tuesdays and Thursdays, a little cocoa, bread and butter in the morning, a little meat at the evening meal; Wednesdays and Fridays, a black fast as in Lent. On Sundays his first meal of the day, after hearing several Masses, was at 2.00; if it was fairly substantial, he ate nothing else that day; if that meal was light he allowed himself cocoa or tea and bread in the evening. On the days he took meat he often asked his sister to cook fish instead; then he would tell her to take the fish home with her and leave the water she used to boil it; he would then dunk his dry bread in the fishy liquid. His sister used to say:

> I don't know how our Matt exists on the small amount of food he eats. Yet, in spite of his fasting he always looked well and healthy and was not emaciated looking. And he was well able to do his work, which was hard work.

When, in his late sixties Matt's health broke down and he had to stay away from work and attend hospital, he ate whatever the doctor ordered, and when in hospital, or in a friend's house, would eat whatever was placed before him. He curtailed sleep to a minimum, usually allowing himself four hours sleep each night and that on a comfortless bed. Like St Francis he allowed 'Brother Ass' no ease. Every Saturday he went to Clonliffe College for confession to Dr Hickey and Dr Hickey visited him in Rutland Street. On a piece of paper in one of his books was written, 'A Prayer for my Spiritual Director'. It is not in Matt's handwriting. Whether Dr Hickey or some previous director wrote it for him we do not know; but we do know that Matt, so truly in earnest about spiritual matters and so well-versed, through reading St Francis de Sales' instructions, would have taken on no penitential practice without first discussing it with Dr Hickey.

His fasts, prayer-filled nights and penances were all traditional, the spiritual heritage St Patrick bequeathed to the Gael. Even in our century, with its cult of comfort, Ireland still retains the world's most penitential pilgrimage, Lough Derg. One exercise of that pilgrimage takes place at St Patrick's Cross. The pilgrim stands, back to the wall where the cross is cut in the stone, and prays with outstretched arms in the ancient *crois-fhighill*, cross-vigil. Mrs Talbot told her daughters that often she woke at night to see Matt praying until 4.00 a.m. with arms out-stretched, but she warned them not to speak of this to anyone outside the family. Several people, including the late President of Ireland, Seán T. Ó Ceallaigh, who as a boy served Mass in Berkeley Road church, saw Matt praying before a crucifix in this manner, especially when he thought himself alone and unseen.

Twelve years after Matt's death Mr Ó Ceallaigh testified to this and described how he came to know Matt during the 1880s and after:

> Sometimes Matt would be waiting outside before the church (Berkeley Road) opened for early Mass. He got to know a few of us altar-boys well and would call us by our Christian names. We always called him Mr Talbot, though he was very poorly dressed and wore the muffler workingmen wore then instead of a collar and tie. He was very neat and clean; sometimes the boys would call him 'Holy Joe' making fun of him, but he never resented that; he was very kind and friendly. He would pray aloud sometimes and seem oblivious of everyone and everything.
>
> Later on, when I was older, he often stopped me in the street to ask how I was getting on at school; and when I started work he would enquire how things were and warn me to mind my work and do it well.

Matt did not have the gift of prophecy and did not foresee that young John Kelly was destined to become a President of Ireland.

5

In Martin's timber yard

Later in his life, when other workmen asked Matt Talbot why he had never married, he replied that it would have interfered with the manner of life he intended to live. His mother told his sisters that he had once considered the matter but decided against marrying. Mrs Talbot was the only person taken into his confidence at the time. He was on building work at the home of a leading Protestant clergyman. The cook there, noticing that he did not flirt or joke with the maids like his workmates, spoke to him one day. She informed him that she had saved sufficient money to buy and furnish a house and ended by proposing marriage. Matt said that he would consider her proposal and pray about it. After making a novena he told the girl, a Catholic, that he had been enlightened and had come to the conclusion that he had better remain single. There is no clue to the cook's identity or to her reaction. Once, when a friend asked him why he had not married, he said that the Blessed Virgin told him not to.

As the 1890s ebbed away Dublin saw many changes. The Gaelic League, Sinn Féin and the movements for industrial and agricultural reform came into being. Dame Nellie Melba, whose singing captivated Dubliners in 1883, paid the city a second visit in 1900 and found it quite different. The first electric tram went from Haddington Road to Dalkey in 1896; only the bravest ventured on the initial run as everyone expected to be electrocuted by the current from the overhead lines. Sir Horace Plunkett caused a sensation by driving his motor-car, then a novel sight, around the Phoenix Park and up and down Sackville Street.

In 1898 the celebrations to mark the centenary of the '98 rebellion took place, causing the embers of patriotism to glow again, if only briefly. The Castle authorities became

In Martin's timber yard

very uneasy again a year later, when the Boer War started, as there was much pro-Boer sympathy in Dublin. On the very streets being decorated for Queen Victoria's visit in 1900 the ballad-singers were singing *Kruger Abu!* to an Irish air:

> The Boers, they were marching
> And the British wanted fight
> The Boers took out their long-Tom
> And blew them out of sight.
> Sound the bugle! Beat the drum!
> Give three cheers for Kruger
> To _____ with the Queen an' her oul' Tambourine
> And hurrah for Kruger's Army.

It was the Queen's fourth visit to Ireland and one who saw her recorded his impressions:

> She was then eighty-one and, as a mark of appreciation of her Irish soldiers, abandoned her annual visit to the south of France, and came to Dublin instead. She stayed for three weeks and was on the whole well received, driving without escort through the streets.... Some people, with a mixture of incredulity and malice not uncommon among us, went so far as to allege that the old lady did not actually realise where she was and believed herself to be in France. I saw her one afternoon outside the Mater hospital, while she listened to an address of welcome, her heavy Hanoverian face rising large and somnolent over the side of the carriage.

The writer, young John Horgan from Cork, was pro-Boer himself, as were many of his fellow-students attending the lectures prescribed by the Incorporated Law Society for solicitors-to-be. In the Gaiety Theatre an Irish play, *Casadh an tSúgáin*, was a startling innovation. So was another play, *The Countess Cathleen*, by W.B. Yeats, for which the beautiful Maud Gonne was practising her part. Arthur Griffith, a

Dublin journalist just back from South Africa, was knee-deep in paper, printers' ink and all the paraphernalia of newspaper production in the little Liffeyside office where the *United Irishman* was struggling to come out weekly and keep clear of debt. The parish priest of Doneraile, Co Cork, Canon Sheehan, was writing popular novels, and in the *Leader* David Moran was tackling such vested interests as the brewing industry, the railways and the music-halls with their stage-Irishmen and jokes borrowed from *Punch*.

Labour was unorganised in Dublin in 1900. Matt Talbot was then working as a ganger with the Dublin Port & Docks Board. On 2 July 150 employees of the Port & Docks and of several shipping lines went on strike for better wages. The late Garry Holohan of Mobhi Road was foreman to a group including Matt who went on strike the first day; their demand was for a rise of sixpence a day on an already miserable wage; by the second week forty-three of the workers under Mr Holohan were out and altogether 500 were on strike. The *Evening Herald* of 9 July reported that workers were to be brought in from England to take the place of the strikers. Riots developed and there were skirmishes between the police and the men on strike; the newspapers carried long lists of men arrested and charged with riotous conduct, but Matt Talbot's name is not on any list. Soon the strikers drifted back in groups. Mr Holohan crossed out the names on his list as they returned, using different pencils for different batches and dates. Four men in his group never returned: Doran, O'Reilly, Mulcahy and Matt Talbot. The latter's stand at this juncture, thirteen years before the big strike of 1913, is worth noting. His attitude to strikes, labour conditions, etc., is discussed in chapter 6.

When the Boer War ended Mr Winston Churchill, fresh from his experiences as a war correspondent in the Transvaal, came to give a lecture in Dublin. He forgot to mention the Irish regiments so his speech fell flat. By that time Matt Talbot had a permanent job at T. & C. Martin's, the timber firm at the North Wall. Over a hundred years

In Martin's timber yard

in business, Martin's was a firm Matt was glad to be in, especially as work did not start there until 8.00. This gave him time to hear several Masses before reporting for work. When first employed there he was in the creosote boiling division; later his job was carrying planks to the sawmills, then he was in the hardwood drying sheds and finally in Castle Forbes yard where Dan Manning had a house and where Mr Carew was foreman.

In the early 1950s, when the first edition of this book was written, I met and interviewed more than twenty men who had worked with Matt in Martin's and knew him well. Since then as many more have been located, the last and probably the man who knew Matt best, Paddy Laird, dying in 1985. Ted Fuller was married to a niece of Matt's old drinking companion, Pat Doyle, and knew Matt for over twenty years. He said:

> When Matt was creosoting timber in the boiling division he had very hard work. It was dirty work, too, as the tar used to spatter on men's clothes and Matt was a very clean, neat little man. His suits were always too big for him, like as if someone gave them to him. I called to his room sometimes; a small bed, a stool, some little holy pictures, a crucifix and holy water font were all he had there. When working in the drying-shed he kept a sack over his shoulders in wet weather. In slack times, while waiting for loads of timber to arrive, I often noticed him kneeling in prayer between the timber-stacks. Because he didn't like to be seen praying, I used to knock a plank, or shout to someone else, or cough, to let Matt know I was coming. He'd rise then and be out to meet me. I was often home from work with him; he'd visit St Lawrence O'Toole's church on the way, then the chapel at St Joseph's, Portland Row. Sometimes I'd go in with him, stay five or ten minutes maybe, but I always left Matt behind me there. 'Thanks be to God,' and 'Praise be to God,'

were frequent sayings of his. He always wore a bowler hat; if he heard men in the yard abusing the Holy Name, he would raise his hat as a gesture of silent protest.

Though Matt was by this time proficient in reading, his hand-writing was poor, likewise his spelling. He had table-books and ready reckoners and other aids in his room and in his hut in Martin's yard to help him make up bills. Ted Fuller was a great stand-by in times of mathematical crisis:

> When he was moved to a job where he had to do calculations, he was upset. He came to me and said, 'Oh, Ted, I don't know will I be able for this. I'm no good at figures. I'm afraid I won't be able to make up the bills for the loads.' So I went round to his room a few evenings and showed him how to figure it out and I told him that I'd be working near him and all he had to do if in a fix was to give me a shout.
>
> Matt used to subscribe to all the workers' funds we had — that was before the Unions started — but he'd always ask a day's grace before bringing the money as he never carried money on him. Later he left money in Mr O'Connor's office and drew on it if asked for something for charity or a sick worker. He often gave men in the yard the price of a pair of boots. All the men had great respect for him. He was very strong on the rights of labouring men and said they should stand up for themselves. 'Fair wages for a fair day's work and the other way around,' he'd say. Bob Laird and his son, Paddy, Michael McGuirk, Dan Manning, Dillon and others knew Matt very well. We were real fond of him. Some men who didn't know him so well, thought him a bit odd; but everyone knew he was sincere and holy, though he tried to hide that side of him. Even Mr McKeag, one of the foremen, who was a Protestant, thought the world of Matt.

In Martin's timber yard

Ted also described the kinds of work Matt did:

> At one time he was in the creosote boilers, where timber was dipped into the boiling tar, very hard work. Later he carried deal timber from the piles to the sawmills; later again he helped Harry Kearney in the hardwood drying shed and after that he was in the part of the yard known as Castle Forbes. He was a topping worker and very punctual; he wouldn't waste a minute. When waiting for a load of timber to arrive he'd avail of that time to pray or read; he always had pamphlets, lives of saints and the like, in his coat pocket.

Joe Nolan commented on Matt's build, which did not help to lessen the hard work he did:

> He was small and it often struck me that carrying the deals either to the stacks or to be creosoted must have been very hard on Matt, for he had the most sloping shoulders of any man I ever saw. You would wonder how he kept the planks from slipping off his shoulder with such a slope.

The late Harry O'Connor, father of John O'Connor, our internationally famous concert pianist, was cashier at Martin's. He corroborated what has been recorded about Matt leaving money in the office and drawing on it when asked for subscriptions to various good causes. He also said that money accumulated to Matt's credit because he would not claim the bonus paid to men for loading or unloading a ship, especially when the captain wanted to catch the tide. If the ship caught the tide each man got two shillings; if it did not they only got their ordinary day's pay. Mr Gethin, a clerk, and Mr Dillon, a foreman, referred to the upset caused by Matt's refusal to accept this special allowance.

For this bonus the men would have to work extra hard and Matt would work harder than any. As it was part of my duty to pay this money it upset my accounts when one man failed to claim. I called Matt to order about it. He said, 'It's true we have to work harder, but then I have many a slack moment in the day, waiting for loads, so I don't feel entitled to this money.' At last he agreed to leave it with me and I put it to his account in Mr O'Connor's office and he used it for charity. His real objection to taking the bonus was because other men who got smaller wages than he did and had harder work to do most days, only got the same bonus as himself. He felt that they should get more, or that he should not receive the two shillings.

Mr Gethin remembered Matt well:

He got on well with his employers but he could never be obsequious to anyone. When I was stock-taking Matt would have to remain on at the works on a Saturday. When finished I'd say, 'Well, Matt, that's the end,' and he'd reply 'There's an end to everything but the one thing.' Sometimes he'd ask me, 'Do you think you are going to live for ever?' There was not much *bonhomie* about Matt, but he was not uncheerful. He was too unworldly to make the sort of jolly companions I used to prefer .... He wanted to make me a 'saint', but I'm afraid he hasn't succeeded.

Mr O'Connor, the cashier, recalled how Matt made a practice of attending charity sermons preached throughout the city and suburbs. He would walk long distances to the churches where they were preached and would withdraw a pound note from the money Mr O'Connor held for him to pay into the collection for which the sermon was preached. Considering the long distances he walked some Sundays, to Howth or Dalkey or Chapelizod, he must have spent several hours without food. Once a popular preacher was to make an appeal for a well-known charity; the church where he was to preach was in a very select district. When Matt arrived the building was packed to the doors. After trying in vain to get in he noticed some people entering by a side door where a collector was making a sixpenny entrance charge. Matt went round there, pound-note in hand; not wishing to 'break' his donation he explained that he had brought no small change. The other, who had probably seen the note and concluded that the man seeking admission was just trying to enter without paying, said, 'Well, you can't get in here.' Matt turned aside and remarked quietly, 'It's the house of God.' However, he remained near the porch and listened carefully to the sermon. One wonders if the collector saw the collection taken up and noted the amount, very large in those times, given by the man he had refused to admit by the side-door.

Paddy Laird of Cabra, who died as recently as 1985, was one of our last links with Matt Talbot. Of all the men who worked in Martin's between 1900 and 1925 he was Matt's closest friend. As a boy he was often sent to Martin's yard with the midday meal for his father who worked there. Bob Laird and Matt used to walk home from work together and when times were bad Matt helped Laird with money. Bread and margarine were often the staple diet of families where the father was on a low wage. Young Paddy disliked margarine and would turn up his nose when it appeared on the table; his parents would tell him, 'Only for Matt Talbot you'd have nothing on your bread; you mightn't even have bread!' Paddy told of an incident that happened when he was about twelve years old:

> I was sent down with the usual little parcel for my father and I rambled off, as I often did, to find Matt in his shed. A rat was on the table nibbling at Matt's bit of dry bread. I was going to peg a stone at it but Matt stopped me. He spoke to the rat, nice and soft

like, 'Come on, now. Get down.' And the rat obeyed him. Then he began to tell me about the good rats do. 'They may do some damage, but they clean the sewers. They are God's creatures. He made them for some purpose.'

A few years later Paddy went to work at Martin's and walked home from work with his father and Matt in the evenings. He did not always relish the prospect because, 'the very evening you'd be in a hurry going somewhere, Matt would want to make a visit'.

> He'd say, 'We'll make a visit,' or maybe he wouldn't say anything at all, just go into St Laurence O'Toole's or Portland Row, and my father and myself wouldn't like but to go in, too. Some people think that Matt would not chat, that he went around in silence. Not at all. He was very pleasant company and enjoyed a laugh. On our way from work he'd join in when we talked about strikes or politics or football matches. Matt never went to a match when I knew him, but he'd listen when you were describing the play and he'd remember the names of the players and their teams, and after the next game they figured in he'd ask how they played. Now that I think back on it, I don't believe that he had any interest himself in sport but he liked to be affable and good company.
>
> The only thing he wouldn't laugh at was a dirty joke, and he'd check men who used the Holy Name when speaking. A strange thing, he could handle bullies; men whom no one would like to cross would be like lambs after a few words with Matt. He picked up some of the slang in use in his time. I remember one, 'Ah, go an' get your hair cut!' If anyone was rushing him at the loading or unloading of the timber Matt would say that in a jolly sort of way. In fact he used it long after it went out of date.

In Martin's timber yard

He was fonder of his sister Mary (Mrs Andrews) than of Susan (Mrs Fylan). I think Susan was a bit bossy. I remember during the First World War, Ned Lyons, a carter in Martin's, was worried when word came that his son Jack was 'reported missing, presumed dead.' That's what was in the telegram, but Matt said to Lyons, 'Don't worry, Ned. He'll be home.' Next day another wire came confirming that Jack was dead; 'Ned,' said Matt, 'Forget that wire.' Sure enough, when Ned Lyons went home that evening, there was Jack sitting in the kitchen. It seems that he had been given leave but no one entered it on the lists of men on leave.

Dan and Mrs Manning, with their children, lived in a house in the part of the timber-yards known as Castle Forbes. they both came to know Matt very well, as did their houseful of little girls. Mr Manning thought Matt the most conscientious workman he ever met:

> He would not waste a moment; when free he'd be praying or reading. Except for the few minutes taking his scrap of lunch he spent his lunch hour at his books or praying. He seemed to have his own way of praying, not reading prayers or saying prayers learned by heart. In spite of his hard penance — my wife can tell you about his lunch — he was well able for his work and looked well. He was a silent man and tried to avoid notice; he went about with his eyes cast down.... I never met anyone like him; he was totally wrapped up in God; but always in good humour and a great favourite with all the men. By arrangement with Mr Carew, the foreman, he opened the gates each morning on the dot of ten to eight. Sometimes he'd get a bit fussed if men were rushing him with orders; if any special difficulty arose he would go to Mr Carew.

The Manning children, Mary, Kathleen, Teresa, Mona and Josie played in the yard and would peep into the hut watching Matt, who thought himself unobserved, at his prayers. Mrs Manning was pleased as 'he was a good influence on them and when free he would tell them stories from the Bible and stories of saints.'

> He always greeted me, when he came with his billy-can, with word of what saint's feast it was that day. He had a special wish for my Tessie (Teresa) as she was called after St Teresa of Avila; that St Teresa and St Catherine of Siena he used to describe as 'great girls'. At that time everyone was talking of 'little St Thérèse' (Thérèse of Lisieux). He said she was 'a real little brick'.
>
> For his midday meal he used take a small drop of tea and cocoa mixed which I used to heat for him, but he would let it get cold before taking it. I never saw him eat, but heard he sometimes had a little dry bread. Once I said he should drink it hot and have milk and sugar on it; but he said he preferred it as it was, 'just for a little penance'. When coming to work and going home he would wear a swallow-tail coat and bowler hat, the coat was too big for him. He changed into working clothes and after work would wash at a tap in the yard and tidy up; he was very particular, if any tar spots got on his clothes he would wash them off; he wanted to be clean because he was going to visit the Blessed Sacrament on his way home.
>
> A little girl named Annie sometimes came to play with my children. When Matt heard her using the Holy Name when playing he reproved her; when she did it again he put her out of the yard, as he had threatened to do the first time she offended. I felt sorry for the child; she later died a very holy death.

Mrs Manning also told how one evening in winter she

In Martin's timber yard

was alone in the house. The yards were closed and everyone, as she thought, had gone home. There was a knock on her back door and, startled, she asked who was there. It was Matt; he explained that he had been 'saying a few prayers and never noticed the time slipping by'. Mrs Manning let him out through her front door.

> Once he found some eggs my hens had laid in the yard and brought them to me. I told him that he shouldn't have bothered but should have kept them for himself. He replied, 'But they weren't mine to keep.' On another occasion I was speaking to him when Mr Martin, the Manager, came along. I felt he might think I was wasting Matt's time and began to move away, but Matt said. 'Stay where you are. Fear no one; there is only One to remember', and he pointed to heaven. I regarded Matt Talbot as a very holy man, and so did all the workmen; and Father John Flood of St Lawrence O'Toole's thought the same.

In an interview Father Flood said that he did not know Matt personally but when he was a curate in St Lawrence O'Toole's he often saw

> a strange figure of a man who always seemed to be in a hurry. He wore a workman's clothes, was spare and ascetic-looking and seemed insufficiently fed. He ran rather than walked, stayed about fifteen minutes in the church in the evenings and also came in the mornings to Mass on his way to work.

Later, in conversation with some parishioners, Father Flood learned that the man's name was Matt Talbot. He was not the only person who noted that Matt ran rather than walked. Patrick Farrell, who knew Matt for over thirty years, remarked, 'Matt could not get enough of the holy Mass. You would meet him running to it.' Pat Doyle, speaking of the Matt Talbot *he* knew, said 'He wanted only the one thing — drink.' John Monaghan, clerk in Gardiner Street church, who often met Matt there, said, 'He would speak if you greeted him, but you had the impression that he would rather no one spoke to him. Matt wanted only the one thing — God.'

John Gunning was a friend of Matt's for over thirty years; he was employed by West's jewellers of Grafton Street as a silver polisher:

> We were both in the Rosary Confraternity of the Dominican Church, St Saviour's. Matt lent me the Life of St Catherine of Siena. Before I read it I asked him if she wore a chain. He looked confused and said he supposed she did. ... Some time later he told me of a devotion to Our Lady, the True Devotion, and said it lifted him from earth to heaven; he said he wore a chain, sign that he made himself a slave of Our Lady. I asked him to get me a chain. He did and brought me to Clonliffe College to Dr Hickey. As Dr Hickey was out we saw Father Waters; he enrolled us and I wore the chain, same as Matt.

As Matt could not have heard of the devotion before 1914 or 1915 this incident did not take place until these dates or later. The chain was 'a small one, about the size of a chain in a clock', according to Gunning. (The chain receives further attention in chapter 10.) The fact that Father Waters enrolled Matt and John immediately seems to indicate that others were enrolling in the devotion at that period.

6

Matt and his union on strike

In 1894 there were fifty-one Irish trade unions, the following year ninety-three, all listed in the British Board of Trade Returns. At early Trade Union Congresses the agenda dealt mainly with grievances such as night work in bakeries, non-union labour being employed by firms engaged on large government contracts, and the practice of employing boys to do men's work. In 1896 James Connolly, a Monaghan man in his middle twenties, was hardly known outside Ulster, though he had been active in the Scottish labour movement and was being spoken of in Dublin labour circles. He founded the Irish Socialist Republican Party and, early in the new century, went to America. Occasionally Dublin workers were visited by another labour leader, James Larkin, whose magnetic personality and great driving force were to become legendary. His own terrible experiences as an exploited youth in Liverpool and elsewhere gave him authority to speak and to get a hearing.

Jim Larkin's first visits to Dublin were to organise the unskilled workers. There was a rather sharp cleavage between the city's skilled and unskilled workers. The former were organised in their Unions and considered themselves a class apart from those without skills, a much exploited lot. Dockers, carters and casual labourers were underpaid by employers and victimised by tenement landlords, money-lenders, publicans and pawn-brokers. The GAA, the Gaelic League and movements for industrial revival such as Horace Plunkett's, meant little to this host of unskilled, unorganised workers. Their attention was perpetually engaged in the grim struggle for existence and they had neither the time nor the heart to engage in any movement for their own betterment. It was this 'submerged tenth' of labour in

Dublin that Larkin aimed at organising.

Matt Talbot, an unskilled worker, belonged to this section of society; being unmarried and, through the ascetic life he had voluntarily chosen, having reduced his material wants to a minimum, he did not perhaps feel the hardships others in the same category did. But he was not insensible to their miseries; it will be recalled that he often bought boots for fellow-workers and he helped the Laird and other families over many a rough patch.

In 1908 attempts were made to form one large union of Irish workers, but these efforts failed. Jim Larkin broke with the Liverpool Union, of which he was Irish representative, and joined the Dublin and Cork workers who were planning a union independent of labour organisations across the Irish Sea. This was the nucleus of the Irish Transport and General Workers' Union. To balance its numerical and financial weakness it had Larkin for General Secretary. Over the next few years the ITGWU was engaged in a series of strikes and lock-outs. One branch was for builders' labourers and one of the first to join it was Matt Talbot. Meanwhile Connolly had returned from America and became Secretary of the Belfast branch of the ITGWU and organiser for Ulster, though relations between him and Larkin were not the best up to 1913, the year that saw the not unexpected clash between capital and labour in Dublin.

Matt being one of the workers to come out when called upon during the 'Great Strike', a brief survey of the conditions and events that led to the strike is relevant. According to the British Board of Trade enquiry in 1912 food prices rose by 14% between 1905 and 1912. However, wages did not rise to meet the cost of living. Writing in *Studies* on this period, the late Seamus O'Farrell answers the obvious question: What did the poor do?

> They ate less and they repatched their clothes. There was nothing else they could do. State assistance, reluctantly given and after imposing degrading

conditions, consisted of admission to the Poorhouse or relief in kind.

Relief in kind, commonly known as Outdoor Relief, meant a few loaves of bread, a pinch of tea, a small dole of sugar, a few ounces of margarine. To get it the recipient had to go personally to the Poorhouse and present a ticket issued by the Relieving Officer. On it a widow and her children had to exist or die. Rent was met by charitable organisations, the Poorhouse being the only shelter the State was willing to provide. The pennies of neighbours buried the dead. They suffered, God knows, and suffered in silence. The law-givers were far away in Westminster, concerned with the demand for Home Rule. The slum owners were represented in the Dublin Corporation. To whom could they appeal? To Caesar, against Caesar?

The poor helped the poor when no other help was available. They gave the bread out of their own hungry mouths to those whose need was greater.... How they lived was nobody's concern but their own. Where they lived was decided for them by the rent of a tenement room. Out of 16 shillings little remained to pay for shelter when a family had been even half-fed.

Dublin, as a manufacturing centre, lacked the advantages which the proximity of coal mines, iron deposits, great forests and other raw materials afforded many cities of the industrial world. On the other hand it had the river which cut the city in two, an indubitable if not fully utilised asset; it also had a plentiful supply of labour, especially unskilled labour, too much indeed for the needs of its industry. It was this disproportion of supply and demand in the labour market that constituted Dublin's gravest economic problem in the decades preceding the Strike.

Sidney and Beatrice Webb, friends of George Bernard Shaw, visited Dublin just before the Great Strike. Shaw, incidentally, was born in the same year as Matt Talbot, his fellow-Dubliner. The Webbs stayed as guests of Horace Plunkett at his home in Foxrock. The Countess of Fingall, related by marriage to Plunkett, was staying there at the time. In her memoirs, *Seventy Years Young*, she wrote:

> The Sidney Webbs came and, true to their Socialism, would not change for dinner. They did a tour of Ireland and Mrs Webb came back to Kilteragh (Plunkett's home) and reported: 'They do not know the beginning of Socialism in this country. Everyone of them is an individualist to his or her backbone.' It was quite true. There is no natural Communism in the Irish character.

In 1913 Larkin organised a strike against William Martin Murphy's Dublin Tramways Company. Murphy owned the *Irish Independent* newspaper. The timing was good, as it was Horse Show Week and Dublin was crowded with titled and wealthy people from Ireland and Britain when the tramway men simply stepped off their trams and left them on the street. Murphy immediately declared that in future he would not employ any ITGWU tramway men. Other employers followed his lead and there were lock-outs all over the city. Larkin retaliated by initiating 'sympathetic strike tactics'; this resulted in workers not previously involved coming out. Martin's men went on strike early in September, Matt Talbot with the rest. Their action followed the riots between police and strikers in O'Connell Street where two workers were killed, hundreds wounded, an old woman trampled upon and people going to or coming from Mass were caught and injured in the mêlée. This happened on Sunday 30 August and that evening and throughout the night a group of constabulary, most of them drunk, attacked blocks of tenements in Corporation Street and Foley Street, batoning the inhabitants, men, women and children, and wrecking the humble houses and poor belongings of the unfortunates living in that area. They then turned their attention to Beresford Place and Ringsend. Misfortunes

Matt and his union on strike

multiplied when two tenements in Church Street collapsed, killing seven people and seriously injuring many others.

It has been stated more than once, and publicly, that Matt Talbot was a strike-breaker who took no interest in his fellow-workers' struggle for better conditions. This is quite untrue. Apart from the statements of men in Martin's, documents still preserved by his union utterly disprove this allegation. Matt joined the Builders-Labourers' Branch on 22 September 1911 and was a fully paid-up member when the 1913 Strike began. He paid the strike levy. He did not carry a picket but neither did he pass one; men in his age-bracket, like Bob Laird, were not asked to picket. If he had 'scabbed' would not the union have expelled him? Yet, his name remained on the books and his Branch paid him National Health Insurance benefit during his illness of 1923-24. At a workers' meeting held during the 1920s a visiting speaker called Matt 'a strike-breaker and a scab'; he was immediately shouted down and forced to withdraw the epithet.

A lot has been made of Matt's non-attendance at union meetings, especially during the Strike; but he never read newspapers or public notices, never raised his eyes when walking along a street except when passing a church; the strike gave him the opportunity — which he gladly availed of — to spend the entire day in the church, mostly in St Francis Xavier's, Gardiner Street. Even today, when the labour movement is highly and efficiently organised, well-educated and articulate members often fail to show up at ordinary or even special meetings.

Several workers and other acquaintances of Matt Talbot gave sworn evidence concerning his attitude towards workers and employers, towards Jim Larkin and his stand during the Great Strike. James Tallon said:

> The 1913 strike troubled me and I asked Matt what were the rights of it. He said that it had worried him, too, but he spoke to a priest in Gardiner Street who

gave him a book to read. In it he read that no one had the right to starve the poor into submission. 'That was enough for me and settled my conscience', he said.

John Robins stated:

> I never heard Matt speak against his employers but he knew quite well that the men were not sufficiently paid. He once described a certain foreman as 'a bosses' man'. He held that a claim for fair pay for a fair day's work was just.

Frank Larkin, no relation of Jim Larkin, said:

> Matt had a great regard for Larkin and for anyone who worked for the good of others. He felt that Larkin had been let down by the men after the strike and spoke of their ingratitude towards their leader.

Matt's brother Joe took an active part in the Strike. After the grim winter of 1913/14 the English unions refused to send any further financial support to the Dublin strikers. These, faced with no alternative but starvation, had to return on the employers' terms; men who had been prominent during the strike were in many cases not taken back. Joe Talbot was among those refused re-employment.

Joe Gethin, the clerk who took Matt to task for refusing to accept the bonus made to workers in Martin's when they had to work extra hard to get a ship loaded or unloaded in quick time, said:

> The reason Matt would not go for his strike pay was because he didn't think he had a right to money he hadn't worked for. He went out on strike with the rest and paid the strike levy. The men did not ask him to come for the strike pay; they brought it to him and to others. He was one of a group nearly sixty years old;

that was the age of retirement then for unskilled workers.

Brother Furlong SJ, the sacristan in Gardiner Street Church mentioned that a formidable lady, a Miss X, was very antagonistic to Matt:

> During the Strike she drew my attention to Matt, who spent most of his time praying in our church. 'I don't wonder,' she said, 'at that old Larkinite,' meaning Matt, 'being on the side of the strikers. He's a socialist and has the socialist catechism in his pocket.' Matt was certainly on the side of the working men whom he thought were unfairly treated. Miss X was the only person I ever heard speaking ill of him and I think she was a bit eccentric. The general opinion of everyone coming to our Church was that he was a very holy man.

Mr McKeag, a Protestant who was a foreman at Martin's, had this to relate:

> In 1913 I once asked Matt what he thought of the Strike; that was before our men were called out. He replied, 'I do not know enough to judge. Jim Larkin knows best.'

The 'old Larkinite' who spent his time during the Strike praying, gave the strike pay brought to him by fellow-workers to the Leahys, the Donnellans, the Mulvannys and to other men with families living in No. 18 Rutland Street, men who were also on strike but whose strike pay was inadequate to feed those dependent on them.

Trade union leaders since Matt's death in 1925 have always given Matt his due. The late Senator Jimmy Dunne left his sick-bed to attend the unveiling of a commemorative plaque at No. 18 Rutland Street. In the course of a moving tribute he said:

Despite earlier detractions it has to be repeated that Matt Talbot was an early and respected member of the infant IT&GWU and shared in its struggles. Trade unionists and particularly men of Matt's Union are proud to be here today. He has left us an imperishable memory and a reminder that life, however hard, is but a passing phase; Matt, one of our own, has passed the way we all travel and directs our minds towards the End which is the real Beginning.

The late Senator Fintan Kennedy, President of the ITGWU, stated in a public address:

> For Matt, virtue did not mean opting out. He was always prepared to face the consequences of full involvement. It is not presumptuous of us to regard him as a founder-member of the Irish Trade Union movement.

In June 1975, the fiftieth anniversary of Matt's death coincided with the annual Trades Union Congress and Father Morgan Costelloe, Vice-Postulator of Matt Talbot's Cause, was invited to speak to the gathering. In the course of his address he said:

> Trade unions are justly proud of members who distinguish themselves in politics, in business or in industry, but your union is unique. You have a former member who is a candidate for the Church's accolade of sainthood. If Rome decides to declare a new workman-saint in the near future, it will be a great honour for Ireland but it will be a particularly great honour for the ITGWU. You supported Matt when he was desperately poor in 1913 and again from 1923 to 1925. He deserves your support yet again and, since you supported many good causes in the past, I appeal to you to officially support his Cause on this, the Golden Jubilee of his death.

That appeal was not made in vain. At the conclusion of the Congress the 400 delegates present, representing 150,000 Irish members, sent a telegram to the Holy See respectfully requesting that the beatification of Matt, 'Our former member', be expedited.

A Derryman, Stephen McGonagle, during his term as President of the ITGWU, described Matt as 'one who stands out as a beacon light for Irish workers'.

Mr John Carroll, who succeeded Fintan Kennedy as President of the ITGWU was formerly that body's Secretary and Vice-President. In the course of a trenchant article entitled 'Matt Talbot and the Seventies', he wrote:

> Matt Talbot was not himself a great social thinker and apparently he did not feel a compulsion to identify openly with the opposition to the social events of his day. But his very presence among working men and women who were more immediately and directly involved in the struggle for social justice can now be seen in retrospect as a balancing force in the industrial and economic conflict. It was a silent but effective injection of spiritual values into the motivations of his fellow-workers.
>
> To boast that Matt Talbot was a trade unionist and a member of the ITGWU, the union I have the honour to serve, and just to leave it at that would be to exploit his name. But to say that his trade union membership clearly stamped him among his fellows as a colleague and a workmate through the years of their economic subjection, is to acknowledge that our Creator finds many ways of imposing His influence and guidance on the activities of those who might be the least of His flock in worldly terms, but who are, as the scriptures tell us, the joy of the Father.
>
> The quality of our contribution to the brotherhood of man must surely be a major factor in the ultimate beatification of Matt Talbot; for even if we were never

to follow his example of Christian charity, the fact that he was among us shows God's intent and, after all, we are only His instruments.

The only person Matt seems to have discussed the Strike freely with was, strange to say, a Member of the Employers' Federation. This man, Ralph O'Callaghan, a brother of Fr O'Callaghan in Berkeley Road Church, to whom Matt went occasionally for confession, was the owner of W. & P. Thompson's, Wine Merchants, 85 Lower Gardiner Street. Mr O'Callaghan had heard his aunt speak of one tenant in No. 18 Rutland Street whose spirit of prayer, love of spiritual reading and penitential life were extraordinary; she asked her nephew to give the man some of his clothes and to lend him some books. So Matt was invited to visit the wine merchant in his home at Windsor Road, Rathmines. After their first meeting Matt visited Mr O'Callaghan three or four times a year, borrowing and returning books or lending books to the other, who seems to have been a deeply religious man. Mr O'Callaghan told of their first meeting:

> I tried to ascertain was he quite normal — free from eccentricity and with common sense on matters concerning religion. He made a most favourable impression on me. He was somewhat shy at first but after a few visits seemed to be quite at home with me and would chat; on a few occasions he accepted a little hospitality. He was very poor in 1912 and 1913 and came regularly until his illness in 1923. In manner he was plain, but natural and unaffected; he was direct and outspoken. I judged him to be shrewd and clear-headed, with a strong will. There was nothing whatever nervy or over-wrought about him, or anything to suggest that he was the slightest bit unbalanced.
>
> His faith, devotion and utter sincerity were apparent in all he said on religious subjects. He freely admitted to intemperance in his youth, saying, 'I was terribly

fond of drink, but God gave me the grace to give it up; it was a great struggle for me.'

They continued to meet as usual during and after the 1913 Strike.

Matt talked very freely to me about the labour situation and the Strike. The subject was a delicate one, since he was a 'striker' while I was an employer and a member of the Employers' Federation with which the strike leaders were at war. I admired his tact during these talks: the bitterness of the controversies was entirely absent. Though he tried not to hurt my feelings he held his own opinion and was well able to do so. He was pleased when the men, who were undeniably underpaid, got a rise in wages, yet he kept himself detached from the high feeling prevalent in the city and certainly did not allow it to interfere with his spiritual life.

Though Matt's activity during the Strike was not very spectacular, it was none the less useful; out of his scanty strike pay he managed to give money to fellow-workers who were harder hit and whose children were threatened by hunger. At no time — before, during or after the Strike — had he ever curried favour with the bosses. He told a friend that he spent the time of the Strike praying and reading. Both employers and employees needed someone to fast and pray for them, for in the heat of the dispute both sides lost sight of the fundamental evil that was bringing Dublin to her doom. The real problem was too many hands for too little work, a problem that had its roots in generations of misgovernment.

The great disparity in Ireland's capital and chief towns was not between Irish employers and Irish workers but between the Irish people and the armies of alien officials, place-hunters, top-heavy garrisons, and the hordes of hangers-on, high and low, who battened upon the populace. All of these must have viewed with satisfaction the divisions caused in Dublin by the Strike. Issues became confused; good men on both sides of the capitalist-labour divide held mistaken opinions; Matt Talbot was not the only man who did not understand all the issues, but few were humble enough to admit that, even to themselves.

While city and country tried to recover from the effects of the Strike, the First World War broke out. At last there was work in plenty for the unemployed and the recruiting offices were busy. The rights and wrongs of small nations were widely discussed. Up and down Dublin streets military bands played 'It's a Long Way to Tipperary' and 'Pack up your Troubles in your old Kit-bag'. Men in Martin's yards saw their sons in khaki, waving farewell from the troopships steaming out by the North Wall. Matt Talbot, who had an Andrews nephew bound for the trenches, would have waved with his work-mates as the boys sailed away, while on the quays a band played 'Come back to Erin'.

7

The Great Strike and after

Having found himself drawn with his fellow-workers into the vortex of industrial dispute, Matt Talbot realised that he needed to equip himself to understand the situation. Dr Hickey was at hand to advise him how to extend his reading beyond spiritual frontiers to more mundane areas, reading more pertinent to the period during and following the 1913 Lock-out. Six Lenten lectures given in Gardiner Street by Father Robert Kane, SJ, had been published in pamphlet form under the title *Socialism*. James Connolly attacked the pamphlet in his essay, *Labour, Nationality and Religion*. As many of the men in Martin's belonged to the Gardiner Street men's sodality, it is reasonable to assume that the pamphlet and Connolly's criticisms of it came in for discussion. Matt bought both the pamphlet and Connolly's essay, which appeared in *The Workers' Republic* published at a later date. He also bought several books on labour, capital, a just wage, strikes and similar issues that were, for workers, burning topics at that time. When unfamiliar names like Marx and Engels were being quoted by many who knew little of one or the other, Matt was slowly familiarising himself with the doctrines of the two German socialist economists. He also read Belloc's *The Church and Socialism,* and noted Belloc's reference to Ponsonby, author of *The Camel and the Needle's Eye*, as 'the most sincere Radical I ever met.'

Larger works acquired by Matt after 1913 were Leon Garriguet's *The Social Value of the Gospel,* Leo XIII's letter on *The Condition of the Working Classes* and two *Catholic Social Catechisms*. In the larger one of these he underlined the chapter headings:

> The Patient
> The Sickness
> The Cause of the Malady
> Unlicensed Practitioners
> Famous Doctor's Diagnosis
> Applying the Remedy

Matt also bought three pamphlets by Father Lambert McKenna, a Jesuit interested in social reform. A date on a piece of paper was marked 22 April 1913; it was the day, shortly before the Great Strike, when Father James Walshe, Director of the men's sodality in Gardiner Street, died. It will be recalled how Matt had often gone to confession to Father Walshe, founder of the Penny Dinners charity, prior to his meeting with Dr Hickey.

When there were arguments in Martin's yard about industrial and social problems the men invariably referred the matter to Matt. They regarded him as being very well-read and valued his judgment. One day such a discussion arose and Matt was called down from Castle Forbes to settle the point at issue. 'I don't know the correct answer to that,' he said, 'but I know where to find it.' Somehow, somewhere, he had heard of a book, *Democratic Industry*, by an American Jesuit, Joseph Husslein. Matt tried all the bookshops but failed to find a copy; Dr Hickey did not know of the book, neither did Ralph O'Callaghan.

Months later when the men in Martin's had forgotten about the discussion Matt joined them at their dinner break. They found this surprising as it was by then an accepted fact that Matt would spend that time praying either in his hut or between the timber stacks. He said he was sorry for being so long in finding the answer to their question, but he had had to write to America to the publishers — P.J. Kennedy in New York — for the book. He had it with him and read the answer to his flabbergasted audience. Then he returned to his own section of the yard. The purchase cost him most of a week's wages. Sections he had marked in this book (in 'Talbot's Box', kept in Archbishop's House, Dublin) include *The Origin of Medieval Guilds, A Scottish Merchant Guild, The First Modern Labour Class, Woman and Child Labour, Social Insurance*. Matt also had a pamphlet by Dr Coffey of Maynooth entitled *Between Capitalism and Socialism* and one by Dr Keane, OP, called *A Living Wage and a Family Wage*.

Besides the books he bought, Matt borrowed from the libraries of his sodality in Gardiner Street and the Third Order Library in Merchants' Quay. He lent books to his fellow-workers, most of whom told him they were not able to understand the writings of Newman and others. Some asked Matt if he really understood such books; he invariably answered that he prayed for enlightenment before reading and invoked the help of the Holy Spirit. The list of books lent by Ralph O'Callaghan to Matt, and which were always returned punctually, is in Appendix III. It amazed Ralph how Matt could understand and discuss intelligently whatever he read. By this time Matt seems to have been accepted by his fellow-workers in Martin's as the Church's spokesman on matters of both doctrine and industry.

Though Matt read so much material in 1913 that hitherto was a closed book to him, he did not neglect spiritual reading. Under Dr Hickey's tutelage he read all Newman's works, also those of Rodriguez and Père Grou. His earlier lives of the saints had been pamphlets or slim volumes; now he read more detailed editions. A favourite of his was Drane's book on St Catherine of Siena and he was very struck by a vision the young saint had in which God the Father addressed her as 'My own daughter, Catherine'. When the First World War erupted in 1914 he bought more books and pamphlets including *Young Men of France and War, Catholicism and Peace, What is Orangeism?* and *The Intellectual Claims of the Catholic Church*. He also bought lives of Irish saints, among them St Columbanus, St Gall and other missionary saints.

Autumn had turned to winter and the German armies had

overrun Belgium and begun their invasion of France when Matt's nephew, the Andrews boy who had enlisted in the British Army, came home on his first leave. He called to see his uncle and laughed when Matt said that he didn't like to see his visitor 'in that uniform', and added, 'I wasn't joking'. The basement of No. 18 Rutland Street was a cold, dull place for the young 'Tommy' on furlough; he would not have come at all only that his mother insisted that he call to see his uncle and grandmother. Matt looked tired and showed little interest in hearing of life in English cities or in the trenches. The young man decided to cut his visit short; his grandmother was asleep in bed and Matt had no fire. As he stood up to leave a sudden compassion for this little man, his mother's brother, moved him to take off the warm pullover, one knitted for the troops by patriotic ladies on the Home Front; he thrust it on Matt, wrung his hand and was off before Matt had time to expostulate or refuse the gift. The garment went unworn until after Matt's death in 1925; it was found by the woman who 'inherited' his apartment, then at the top of No. 18; she treasured it as a memento.

Later that winter Matt's mother died. She was almost eighty and had been an invalid during her final years, but was well looked after by Matt and her daughters who called daily while Matt was at work. Other tenants in the house described her as a very quiet old woman who prayed a lot. After her death Matt asked the landlord, a Mr Kelly, to allow him to change to an attic, at 'the top front' of the house. The change was easily made. All his mother's belongings were given to his sisters while he made a couple of trips up the rickety stairs with his few sticks of furniture. It was not much of a load; a man intent on his journey to God travels light. His possessions consisted of a bed-frame, with wooden plank and pillow, a billy-can, his library and the box that housed it ('Talbot's Box'), a crucifix, a statue of Our Lady and a collection of small religious pictures. There was hardly a happier man in Dublin than Matt, 'a man of no property', alone in his attic room. He was poor indeed, but wealthy in true wisdom and never lonely, for in God he lived, moved and had his being. When a neighbour complained to him of her loneliness since the death of someone dear to her, Matt exclaimed, 'But how could anyone be lonely with Our Lord in the Blessed Sacrament?'

His prayer-books of 1914 and 1915 contained scraps of papers with headlines of disasters — Allied losses, German losses — showing that the war caused him some anguish. To him the numbers of fatalities were important in that they meant souls to be prayed for. Men for whom Christ died were being hurled into eternity, perhaps unprepared. Small nations, whose rights were much in the news at the outbreak of war, were forgotten as the conflict gathered momentum. However, in the conflagration that lit Europe, one small nation began to seek a way to right her ancient wrongs.

While Matt and his mother lived in the basement, there was plenty of room and Dr Hickey and Matt could chat quietly in Matt's room while Mrs Talbot slept in hers; now that Matt had the attic room to himself he and his director were more at their ease. They discussed the books Matt was reading, Matt was advised about his austerities and they sang hymns together. Tenants in rooms near Matt's often heard him and his visitor singing together; as Dr Hickey had 'not much of a singing voice', Matt compensated for him, though his voice had lost its volume now that he was almost sixty. By 1914 he had completed thirty years of prayer, sobriety and penance. Though Dr Hickey visited him usually twice a week since his mother's death, Matt still went to confession to him in Clonliffe every Saturday.

Ted Fuller called around occasionally on evenings he knew Dr Hickey would not be there. Mrs Fylan said to him, 'You must have the four-leaved shamrock to be so lucky as to get in. Matt doesn't let anyone in, as a rule. If anyone knocks he only opens the door a few inches. Sometimes I come in during the daytime to see if he keeps it clean; but he got a bit vexed with me because I ran up his gas bill.' Each night when Matt saw Ted about to leave, he would proceed to fill a basin with cold water:

> When I'd be gone he would wash his feet. He did that every night on account of going to Holy Communion every morning. All people, or most of them in my generation, did that, remembering what Our Lord did at the Last Supper, washing the apostles' feet, and out of respect for the Blessed Eucharist. We wouldn't be going daily, like Matt, to the altar, but most of Martin's men were in Gardiner Street sodality and in Father James Walshe's time and after him, Father Tom Murphy's time, they'd be receiving once a month and would wash their feet the night before.

There were many tenants in No. 18 Rutland Street and all called Matt *Mr* Talbot. The Donnellans, the Mulvannys, the Leavys, the Breslins — all of them with families — and Mrs Sweeney in the basement. Frank and Mary Donnellan had a large family and lived nearest to Matt who helped them not only during the strike but again in 1916 when Frank was often prevented from going on night shift because of military curfew. Each Christmas Matt had presents for the Donnellan children and children of other families in No. 18, as well as for the Manning children in Castle Forbes. The presents were thruppenny and sixpenny bits wrapped up in pieces of paper. He often gave Mrs Donnellan ten shillings, saying, 'Don't worry about paying that back. You've a big family. Mind your health, your family needs you.' When she told him how she worried about one son who was constantly getting into trouble, Matt said, 'He's a bit wild, but he's young. Wait and see; he'll turn out to be the best of your boys yet.'

On one occasion when a Donnellan child fell ill, Mrs Donnellan's sister came and they took turns sitting up with the sick child. At about 2.00 a.m. the mother was shaken awake by her sister who seemed very frightened. 'I hear a strange sound like someone singing softly. Is this house haunted or what is it?' The other woman reassured her: 'It's only Mr Talbot in the top front; he prays and sings hymns most of the night.'

Another tenant was Mrs Breslin, known to everyone by her maiden name, Mollie Malone. Like her legendary namesake she was a street trader who

> — wheeled her wheel-barrow
> through streets broad and narrow —

and sold apples, oranges, cabbage, onions, and 'lovely William pears', doing good business along Summerhill and Parnell Street. Unfortunately her husband, Harry, was 'a gambler and fond of the drop'; if left in charge of the barrow he was liable to make off with the takings during his wife's absence. Matt Talbot was not only a customer but a trusted friend. He would mind the barrow and keep an eye on Harry while Mollie dashed home for a cup of tea and to see if the children were all right:

> Sometimes he would buy apples or oranges for young kids he knew; or he'd buy a couple of onions — Carlow onions, not Spanish onions, you understand. He was a jolly man though he had little to say. He never said he was going to the church, though he'd wait and mind the stall for me while I ran home. I used to break up my orange boxes for him but when I'd take the bits to his room he'd only open the door a few inches, thank me and take them in. I used to have my little Madge sitting on the ground under the stall until Matt said, 'It's very cold for that child sitting there; I'll make a little stool for her,' and so he did. A woman in a shop gave me an old shelf and he made the stool from that.
>
> My Harry used to drink and bet and run off with my money when minding the stall; I'd be gone for my tea.

So I asked Matt to stay when I'd be gone. He did. When I'd come back he'd whisper, 'Mollie, he had the money in his pocket', or sometimes, 'Mollie, he took two bob and is gone'. Matt was no Holy Joe. When I'd be complaining about Harry he'd say, 'Ah, don't be too hard on him. At least he won't take his boots off and sell them for drink, as I did in my young days.'

Matt seldom referred to drink but Michael McGuirk heard him once offer a workmate the price of a drink, saying, 'A pint of porter never did anyone any harm.'

Another workmate, Paddy Laird, dismissed the idea that Matt was uninterested in politics:

Sometimes he would call to our house at the time of the First World War. Himself and my mother were on opposite sides. He used to back the Germans and was against the British while the mother would argue against him, she was a real Redmondite. But he would see both sides of any question. 'The English were never good to us, but they have souls; we should pray for them.' He belonged to some association praying for the conversion of England. In earlier years he didn't fast as severely as he did later, and he liked a bit of sweet cake. He seldom spoke about religious matters to me, except to give me books on lives of saints. I often saw him kneeling in prayer in a corner of the timber yard where no one could see him, or between the timber stacks. I used feel ashamed to interrupt him. After a while I'd call him by name and he'd call back, 'What do you want?' He'd come out but would look a little annoyed because he used to hide the fact that he prayed so much.

Some of the men called him a Holy Joe and a diehard, they knew he was against the British you see, but Matt would only laugh and say, 'I'll die with my boots on.' It was another bit of slang he had picked up. He got me to join the Jesuit sodality he was in in Gardiner Street and was my 'sponsor' there. I can't explain the effect he had on me, you felt you were near someone holy and different from the rest of us, yet a worker like us.

Although Matt would discuss politics during the First World War when he visited Bob Laird's house, he avoided the subject in the home of his sister, Mrs Andrews. He would say, when there, 'No politics, now; mind God and no politics.' That was because one of the boys was fighting in France at the time and he feared that a discussion on the rights or wrongs of the war might cause dissension. However, the 1916 Rising and its aftermath was a different story. He would discuss the happenings with Bob and Paddy Laird on their way home from work. Once he referred to the executions of the leaders and the wholesale arrests and deportations that followed, and remarked, 'Our lads will now be all driven into secret societies', a comment as shrewd as it was far-seeing.

From 1916 on he bought the *Catholic Bulletin* regularly. A monthly publication, it was edited by the redoubtable *Sceilg* (J.J. O'Kelly) and published by Gills of O'Connell Street, the long-established publishers of Catholic and nationalist books and journals. The *Bulletin* came in for more than its share of attention from the British forces in the post-Easter Rising period, its offices being raided regularly. Moreover, one issue, having had some articles suppressed by the Censor in Dublin Castle, appeared with every page blank as evidence of the suppression.

A well-thumbed copy, that of November 1916, was among Matt's purchases. The editorial demanded that before England attempted to restore order in Ireland, Dublin Castle and its officials should be set in order first. The Bishop of Cork, Dr Cohalan, contributed a long comment on *Rerum Novarum*, an Encyclical of Pope Leo XIII. A copy of this Encyclical had been bought by Matt in 1913 or 1914 in pamphlet form and he was familiar with it. One article in this copy was marked; it carried names, photographs and thumb-nail sketches of four men. For Matt that article was a quadruple mortuary card. Like Pearse's *Mother*, he would 'speak their names in his own heart in the long nights'. These were the names he remembered:

> GERARD KEOGH, aged twenty, pupil of Synge Street and St Enda's, member of the Holy Family Sodality in Rathmines. The son of a Fenian, he had served with the Fianna before joining the Volunteers. On Easter Monday Pádraig Pearse sent him to Larkfield for a contingent of sixty men. On the way he stopped at Clarendon Street Carmelite church for confession; returning at dawn, he was shot dead outside Trinity College, receiving five wounds.
>
> FRED RYAN, aged seventeen, not long left High Street National Schools, had been a member of the Irish Citizen Army and was in Liberty Hall day and night the week before the Rising. He was killed while bravely endeavouring to cover the retreat of his comrades at the corner of Harcourt Street and St Stephen's Green on the Thursday of Easter Week. He was a member of the Sodality in St Audoen's, High Street.
>
> PETER WILSON, aged forty, from Swords, who was detailed for service at Finglas on Easter Monday, got confession on the nearby golf links on his way to take up duty. He was fighting under Captain Sean Heuston along the Quays on Easter Tuesday when he was killed. His mother is still (in November) making pathetic enquiries to know if anyone can tell what became of his remains.
>
> JACK O'REILLY, a thirty-four-year-old Tralee man, a technical instructor, went early in life to New Zealand and qualified as a civil engineer. He became principal

of the Technical Schools in Tonga (the Friendly Island), and each Christmas the King of Tonga sent to Jack, then Principal of Ballinasloe Technical School and Technical Instructor for all County Galway, a card with a wish, 'To my beloved brother, O'Reilly. Live for ever!' After the Rising he was arrested and imprisoned, first in Dublin, later in Frongoch; he was released in ruined health and died of pernicious anaemia a few weeks later.

The November *Bulletin* also contained some verses smuggled out of Frongoch. The last line of each verse was in Irish. Matt was evidently making some efforts to learn Irish as he had booklets with lessons by O'Growney and cuttings with phrases that someone clipped for him from a newspaper then featuring a series of Irish lessons.

In 1917 the Director of the Men's Sodality in Gardiner Street was a Father Tom Murphy; his family could claim relationship with the famous Father Murphy of Boolavogue and the 1798 Rebellion, so he was attuned to what Bryan MacMahon calls 'the Bugle in the Blood'. He was a fine preacher, drawing and holding great congregations. Faith, patriotism and old, almost forgotten, traditions were the stops he played upon to help his listeners remember their heritage, to encourage them to recover and preserve it.

Matt had recruited as sodality members not only Paddy Laird, but many others of Martin's including, said Michael McGuirk, 'Mr S____ the heaviest drinker in the whole north city, whom he won to sobriety.' Paddy Laird remembered mornings after the Sodality when Matt would ask someone in Martin's yard, 'Were you in Gardiner Street last night? Father Tom was better than ever, it would do you good to hear him.' Men would come who had little inclination for sermons, but who were not averse to hearing about the events that were stirring the capital and the country as a whole. Once Father Murphy had won their attention, they listened readily when he went on to speak on his two favourite religious themes, the Eucharistic Christ and devotion to Our Lady, and after 1918, evoking enthusiasm and support for the newly formed Maynooth Mission to China, since renowned as the Columban Fathers.

8

A poor man helps the poor

On 10 October 1918 the mail boat, *The Leinster,* on her way from Kingstown to Holyhead, was sunk by a German submarine with the loss of 501 lives. The news cast a gloom over Dublin, particularly on men working on or near the docks. In Martin's yards anyone known to be sympathetic to the 1916 men was automatically branded pro-German; one man named Kerr got some abuse and Matt Talbot was called a 'Fianna scout', implying that he was recruiting or encouraging young lads to join Countess Markievicz's *Fianna Éireann.* Among Matt's purchases at the time were *The Plot, German or English? The Nationalist Case Stated* and he also bought the *Catholic Bulletin* regularly. He marked an article on the Lough Derg pilgrimage in the November issue with a leaflet. This was one of the leaflets given to pilgrims on their arrival at Lough Derg and suggests that at some time Matt may have made the pilgrimage; in his copy of the *Bulletin* he had this passage marked:

> At Lough Derg the spirit that gave its ascetical strength to the lives of Ireland's ancient saints lives on. There is heard the ring of the anvil and the hammer that fashioned Columba, Killian, Columbanus, Colman and all the other saints of our race who won back to Christianity a Europe lapsed into barbarism.... There the frugal chastening bread is eaten, the water of repentance is drunk, the bare, cruel rocks crunch the feet, the vigil that carved dark lines beneath the sleepless eyes of our early saints is still maintained — almost all the essential elements of the asceticism that distinguished them still survive.

While the modern pilgrimage to Lough Derg is not as austere as in the medieval or renaissance periods, it is still uniquely penitential in a world where pilgrims' travel is made easy and pleasant and where the exercises at holy places, though devotional, retain little bodily penance. Christian self-denial and self-discipline are not exactly the same, as St Paul explained to the Corinthians when he referred to how their athletes trained — 'they for an earthly crown, we to gain one that is everlasting' — the motive underlying the bodily discipline was the important factor. The physical fitness needed to enable the athlete to excel at the games spurred him to self-denial. Others kept the body in subjection either to strengthen will-power, or to let the intellect benefit from the energy diverted to and canalised in it. St Paul saw mortification not as an end in itself but as a means whereby Christians might conform themselves, in small things as in great, to the likeness of Christ and the will of God.

This was the driving motive of Matt Talbot's fasts and vigils. In terms of his own life he translated Christ's words: 'If any man love me, let him deny himself, take up his cross and follow me.' Holiness is nothing if not diverse in its manifestations. All times, all nations, all creeds and classes have recognised it. Yet it is rare, so rare that when it is encountered, some wonder and admire while some are scandalised. Living with a spiritual intensity far deeper than that of his fellow man, Matt was always 'seeking the things that are above', so he freed himself from anything that entangled his spirit and held him back.

His first step in self-denial was the hardest, as he told John Robins — he had a desperate craving for drink in the three months of 1884 after he took his first pledge. Though he had a longer struggle to rid himself of the tobacco habit, he found a way of overcoming his longing to smoke. He carried a white pebble in his pocket and when John Robins or Ted Fuller filled their pipes and lit up, Matt popped the pebble into his mouth and sucked it while the others puffed away. His closest friends all remarked on this, a practice which Matt abandoned when smoking lost its lure for him.

In June 1920 Maynooth College students listened eagerly when the first letters from the Maynooth missionaries who had left for China a few months earlier began to arrive. It was one bright record in a sad year. The political situation had deteriorated. The new National Parliament, Dáil Éireann, was declared an illegal body; troops were moved in to a country which, according to the *Westminster Gazette*, 'was administered like a country invaded in time of war'. Balbriggan was sacked. The Lord Mayor of Cork, Tomás MacCurtain, was murdered by Crown forces in the presence of his wife. His successor, Terence MacSwiney, said in his inaugural speech, 'It is not those who can inflict most, but those who suffer most, who will conquer.' The Black and Tans came in March, the Auxiliaries in August. Lord Mayor MacSwiney died on hunger-strike in Brixton prison on 25 October and thirteen people were killed and several injured on Sunday 21 November when lorry-loads of Black and Tans opened fire on defenceless spectators at a hurling match in Croke Park.

Matt Talbot bought *The Case against the Promised Boundary Commission* and got cuttings from John Robins, Ted Fuller and Paddy Laird — newspaper reports of killings and photos of De Valera and other leaders. He ran risks going out to early Mass while the curfew was on that winter. Mrs Donnellan tried to dissuade him. 'Almighty God doesn't expect you to risk your life like that, Matt', she said, but she might have saved her breath; curfew or no curfew Matt would be in his usual place in Gardiner Street church, day in, day out. However, one morning in April 1921, he ran into trouble going from Mass to Martin's yard. Matt, never late for work, had been given charge of opening the gates at about a quarter or ten to eight. As he hurried down Lower Gardiner Street, his thoughts, no doubt, were centred on Archbishop Walsh, whose remains were lying in state in the Pro-Cathedral and for whom the Masses in Gardiner

Street had been offered.

On Wednesday 13 April at precisely 7.45 a.m. an explosion rocked the area adjoining Martin's yards. The IRA had blown up the London and North Western Railway Hotel at the North Wall where a force of a hundred Auxiliaries and 'Tans were sleeping. As reported in the Dublin daily newspapers and in the *Daily Mail* of 14 April 1921, Major Ryan, the Black and Tan officer in charge, had ordered his men when they took over the hotel at Easter to 'keep the pavements clear and make all pedestrians pass on the roadway'. This order could enable his men, billeted in the hotel, 'to superintend matters at the North Wall, to examine boats with a view to discovering ammunition, to detect spies coming in etc.'

The moment the explosion occurred Ryan ordered the British troops to comb the vicinity. They came out firing, some still in their pyjamas. One of the first arrested was Matt Talbot, caught opening up Martin's yard. He was brought, with hands up, from his hut in Castle Forbes to the entrance gate, placed against a wall and searched; he was then released. Later that morning when he met Mrs Manning from the gate lodge, he made no reference to his adventure and when she tried to discuss the explosion with him, he changed the subject. The *Daily Mail* and other papers next day carried reports of the bombing and gave a list of casualties: Killed, a man, unknown, said to be one of the attackers. Wounded: Thomas Walsh, 19 Mark Street, James Shaw, 2 Ralph Place and Temporary Cadet Bodie.

American sailors on the New York steamer *Honolulu* witnessed the explosion, the subsequent firing and incidents. They said that all the hotel windows were shattered. 'There was a wild stampede of dockers passing to work; they ran for safety to the Railway Stores nearby; two of them were hit by bullets, and, to add to the commotion, the women-folk of men working in the area all ran to the place.' Many men lost half a day's pay. A search among the newspapers of 14 April does not show Matt

A poor man helps the poor

Talbot in any photos taken, a woman and child hurrying by in the roadway being the only civilians to come within camera range.

Several men in Martin's tried to draw Matt out on the morning's happenings, but he kept quiet about his arrest, though a few had seen him being placed against a wall and searched. By this time the struggle for freedom was at its height and the round of reprisals and counter-reprisals ended with the truce called in June and the talk of an Anglo-Irish Treaty. Though the events of the five years from 1916 to 1921 must have stirred him as an Irishman and touched his life as a citizen of Dublin, they made little or no impact on his inner life. That life, silent, intense and hidden, continued to expand and grow; it surged strongly into every phase of his natural life, Matt Talbot's human existence flowing into and mingling with his interior life as the river with the sea.

His reading during the last decade of his life, 1915 to 1925, included many books on controversial subjects. He was in his sixties and the titles of books and pamphlets he bought at this period suggest that he had been asked questions either by persons who expressed doubts on matters of faith, or by non-Catholics and that he was making sure of the right answers. A list of these is given in Appendix IV. In a book, *Christ among Men*, a translation from Sertillanges, Matt marked the section headed 'Jesus and Nature'. In a compilation entitled *Question Box of the Paulist Fathers*, published in the United States, he underlined two questions: *Must Catholics believe that the world was created in six days?* and *Why does the God of Truth permit so many false religions? The Perfections and wonderful works of God* is a title that indicates the direction his prayer was taking at this period.

Wages had risen in Martin's as in other firms since the 1913 strike, tradesmen receiving proportionately more than men without skills. Matt was still an unskilled labourer. He lacked the training that equipped others to do the kind of work that affords some pleasure, e.g. a carpentry job well finished. The satisfaction of achievement that repays, wholly or in part, the trouble involved in bringing the work to completion was not for Matt. Hundreds of men could have done his humble tasks, the only qualifications required being physical strength, endurance and the will to work. As has been seen, he had another occupation, a hidden one in which, apprenticed to Christ the Master Craftsman, he had acquired skill and found lasting joy. The rise in wages, though not a lot, was welcomed by him as a means of extending his charity. Martin's men, men in his sodality, neighbours in Rutland Street were not the only ones he helped. Every local and diocesan appeal found him ready to respond.

Martin's foreman in Castle Forbes was Mr Carew. He recalled how a Father Duffy from Tullyanna, Monaghan, called and asked permission to take up a collection from the workmen. Mr Carew told him to put up a notice saying that he could call on pay-day to take donations from the men for the charity he represented. On the Friday, when the men were paid, the priest returned and made his collection. Mr Carew takes up the story:

> When he was leaving I asked him if he had been up with Matt Talbot in Castle Forbes, knowing that Matt would be a certain subscriber. He had not known about that part of the yard and went up. Later he came back to me and said 'I scruple about taking what the man up there gave me.' I asked him how much Matt had given him. 'All he had in his pay-packet', said the priest. Matt's pay-packet that day contained £3 1s 6d.

He left generous offerings in Gardiner Street church to buy flowers for the altars; once a week he sought out an old woman, 'gone in the head', who used sit in doorways smoking a pipe, and press money into her hand. From 1920 on he seems to have concentrated most of his almsgiving on the Foreign Missions, particularly the Maynooth Mission to China and the Holy Ghost missions in Nigeria. Over many years he sent subscriptions to the Poor Clares in Newry. A search in the convent records does not show the name Matt Talbot, but the dates of donations coincide with acknowledgement leaflets sent by the nuns to 'A friend in Dublin.' Matt probably sent the money through Dr Hickey or someone else, as he did in the case of other charities he assisted.

Acknowledgements also came from St Joseph's Union, New York (Father Drumgoole's famous orphanage), from an association for the Preservation of the Holy Shrines in Palestine, now Israel, and from a confraternity of St Michael the Archangel in France, probably at the Mont-St-Michel shrine in Normandy. He was in a confraternity in the rue de Sèvres, Paris; members of this body undertook to spend one hour each month praying for the dying. He became a subscriber to the Holy Ghost Fathers' *Missionary Annals* and to the *Far East*, the monthly run by the Columban Fathers, as the priests of the Maynooth Mission to China came to be known. The only letter Matt Talbot ever wrote was in their possession until Pope Paul VI, who thought highly of Matt, requested it for the Vatican Library. Matt had been contributing to the Columban missions in the far east since 1920 through a friend, William Kilbride of Eccles Street. On 7 December 1928, Mr Kilbride sent £3 from Matt Talbot and £1 from himself, with a request that their names would not be published. As the writer was leaving Dublin for some time, he asked that the donation be acknowledged to Matt Talbot, No. 18 Upper Rutland Street; he also suggested that the Fathers ask Matt to pray for the success of their mission:

> I know that he does so already, but still I think that a request from you would come with greater force; and I know no one, cleric or lay, whose prayers I would sooner have.

From that time until 1923 Matt sent, in all, £37 to this missionary society, through Mr Kilbride. (His own letter is reproduced on p. 106). Interrogated, the men who knew Matt best calculated that he never kept more than ten shillings a week for his own needs.

Phil O'Neil, in his book, *Twenty Years of the GAA*, published in 1925, described the year 1922 as 'the year no sincere Irishman can write of without feelings of regret and humiliation', while Pádraig Puirséil, in his work on the GAA, wrote, 'The "terrible beauty" born at Easter 1916 became more and more terrible, and far less beautiful.' The Civil War began in June of that year when friend fought friend while brother killed brother. Cathal Brugha died fighting in July. Arthur Griffith, who never fired a shot, died in August of a heart attack. In August, too, those fellow-fighters and old friends, Harry Boland and Michael Collins, now ranged on different sides, were killed.

The strange friendship between Matt Talbot and Ralph O'Callaghan, the wine merchant, continued throughout all this upheaval. Matt made the journey to Rathmines regularly, books were exchanged and discussed. Once, Matt turned up on a cold winter evening without a top coat. 'Where's the coat I gave you last time you were here?' asked O'Callaghan, somewhat annoyed not to find Matt wearing it. Matt mumbled that he needed money for a charitable purpose, so he had sold the coat. On another evening, 'just to see what he would say', Ralph remarked, 'Matt, you have been granted great spiritual gifts; but you know there's a danger attached to them; you might take pride in them.' Matt replied, 'And why would I? The credit isn't due to me but to God who gave the grace. How little I do, compared with all the great saints.'

In his final years he preserved the same spirit of independence, the same impartiality that he showed when dealing with fellow-workers, with managers or with customers. Michael McGuirk told of how Matt dealt with a 'slippery customer':

A poor man helps the poor

One day a customer came with an order to Matt; he asked him to 'rob' — that was a term we had when a man asked for superior timber while presenting an order for cheaper stuff. Matt refused. The customer then cursed and swore at Matt; he said, 'By ..., if I gave you half-a-crown you'd give it to me quick enough,' meaning the better timber. With that Matt put down the man's docket on his desk and walked away without saying one word. That customer didn't try it on again. He was a big, tough man and I suppose he thought that Matt being so small would be afraid to refuse him.

Michael McGuirk also recalled an incident that happened one day when Matt was praying between the timber stacks while waiting for a load. One of the directors was showing a distinguished visitor around and, hearing some movement in the timber, called, 'Come out, whoever you are in there and don't be afraid.' Matt walked out and said, 'With all respects to you, sir, I never yet met a man I was afraid of.' On another occasion the same director asked Matt if he had seen another worker who had come in late. Matt replied, 'I wish you would not ask me questions like that, questions I do not wish to answer.' When the director passed on Matt turned on the culprit, one Christy Coyle, who had been hiding nearby. 'Did you hear that? Keep it in mind and attend to it. I won't tell a lie to save you or anyone.'

Christy was in his late twenties and liked to try and shock Matt by pretending to be 'a bit wild and living it up'. Matt got him to join the Gardiner Street men's sodality but he often missed meetings; Matt would remark on his absence and ask why he wasn't there. 'Oh, the sodality! Sure I was at the Tivoli last night', and he'd describe the stage show to Matt, exaggerating and embroidering as he went on. The other would continue working and finally say, 'Christy, you're a right boyo, that's what you are. I hope you go to your duties regularly.' Michael McGuirk also told how Matt tried to influence others he knew:

Matt was always trying to get men off the drink. He converted Mr S _____, just by keeping on saying to him, 'What I could do, you can do with God's help.' He'd say the same to me, to Fuller and to Carew, trying to get us to take up some of his fasts and devotions. One man, a coal porter, used to use shocking bad language to his wife when the poor woman brought him his dinner. Matt heard him abusing her, walked over, laid his hand on the man's shoulder and said 'You are crucifying Christ.' From that day out the coal-porter was a changed man.

Several men in Martin's mentioned how Matt brought a man back to the sacraments, a man who had been away for thirty years. They said that Matt brought him to Dr Hickey one Saturday when he himself was going to Clonliffe for his weekly confession. Though his fellow-workers sometimes poked fun at him, calling him Holy Joe or Old Diehard — this last because he admired Mr De Valera — they respected him. Only one man, in an interview, said, 'Matt was a bit of an odd-ball. A loner. As odd as two left boots.' Those who knew him best said, 'We loved him.' A foreman recalled that whenever the weather was bad and he saluted Matt with 'That's a bad day', he got the reply, 'Every day that God sends is a good day', an attitude he retained even when his health deteriorated.

9

Sick, suffering and unemployed

On 5 June 1923 William Kilbride, who was a native Irish speaker, wrote to Fr Dan Coneely, the Editor of the *Far East* magazine. He mentioned Matt:

> Abair paidir beag le h-aghaidh Talbóid atá i droch sláinte. Tá sé ana-carthannach agus níl sé ach ina sclábhuidhe. (Say a little prayer for Talbot who is in bad health. He is very charitable, although only a working man.)

Later that year Kilbride wrote again:

> Tá feabhas mór ar Mhac Uí Talbóid ach ní féidir leis aon obair a dhéanamh fós. (Mr Talbot is greatly improved but is unable to do any work yet.)

During 1923 Matt spent two periods in the Mater hospital, from 19 June to 17 July and from 10 September to 17 October. Professor Henry Moore was Senior Physician at the Mater and Professor of Medicine at University College Dublin. He was one of several witnesses who came forward to testify at the tribunals set up after Matt's death to enquire into his life. The doctor first came to know Matt when the latter came to see him before being admitted as a patient to the hospital in June 1923. Having diagnosed that Matt Talbot was suffering from a kidney and heart condition, he advised him to come into hospital for treatment. With great reluctance Matt allowed himself to be persuaded into doing so. The doctor stated:

> I got the impression that he was quite indifferent to his ailment and was prepared to accept whatever it pleased God to send him. While in hospital he behaved wonderfully as a patient and in a saintly manner. It occurred to me first that he might be a religious crank. I gathered that he gave away a good deal of his money to others, and I had the impression that he left himself short of food. He also told me that he got up at 5.00 a.m. to go, fasting, to an early Mass and told me, too, that he remained in the church for several Masses.

Continuing his evidence Dr Moore said that the disease from which his patient suffered, while not painful in the ordinary sense, would give rise to considerable discomfort. In Matt's case it would have caused shortness of breath if he hurried or climbed stairs, and difficulty in breathing would make it hard for him to sleep. The doctor did not think that Matt looked well, but neither did he look emaciated; his illness would account for this, the bodies of patients affected in this way being inclined to store fluid. Dr Moore gave evidence at both the 1931 and 1948 tribunals.

> I was not long in changing my opinion of Matt Talbot. He was a most obedient and submissive patient and impressed me very much; he was one of the gentlest men I have ever come across and, were it not that I was so busy at that time, I would like to have had him as a friend.
>   It was with some reluctance on his part that I was able to glean from him the information about his life and austerities. I remember advising him to have something to eat after one Mass before going out to hear other Masses. I am fairly certain that he came back to me after his discharge from hospital, but now, over twenty-five years later, I cannot say how often he returned or when he came for the last visit. Of all the persons I have met in my life, Matt Talbot seemed to

Sick, suffering and unemployed

me to be an outstandingly holy man.... Now I have a little talk with Matt every day in my prayers; I have great affection for him and when praying I ask him to do things for me. My son developed infective hepatitis; I got a tiny portion of Matt's wooden pillow from the Archbishop (Dr McQuaid), pinned it to the boy's pyjamas; he began to improve at once and within three days was back at UCD.

It will be noticed that Dr Moore made no mention of Matt wearing chains; neither did two men who were fellow-patients of Matt and in beds on each side of him. The ward sister, Sister M. Veronica Frost, was in charge of St Lawrence's Ward when Matt was admitted. He was fairly ill and two days after arriving he received the Last Sacraments; in 1923 these included confession, Holy Communion and the anointing now called the Sacrament of the Sick. On 2 July he was transferred to St Brendan's Ward and the care of Sister M. Emmanuel. She found that his pulse rate was abnormal, 160 per minute. He was allowed up but instructed to rest during the day on a couch in the hospital corridor. The Sister remembered that he lay with his face to the wall when in the corridor; she had the impression that he was praying and took no interest in what went on around him. When able to walk a little, he said his rosary as he walked, but hid the beads from the sight of others. Heart patients had to ask permission to use the lift when going up to the chapel, and Matt asked permission often; he was forbidden to kneel so he sat silent and motionless on the back seat.

He said nothing about his spiritual life; indeed he hardly spoke at all. I had a nickname for him — 'Poor old Tach' — this was from his ailment, Tachycardia. A young Sister was studying for her exam at that time and said to me, 'I can't remember the anatomical structure of the sternum and chest cavity.' I told her to go and examine 'poor Tach', that his ribs and breastbone were easily studied. For of all the patients I ever saw Matt Talbot was the least covered with flesh.

Men from Martin's came to visit Matt; a Mr Watt came very often. On 17 July Matt was discharged but eight weeks later he had to be re-admitted. This time he was back again with Sister Veronica in St Lawrence's Ward. Her evidence was as follows:

> When fit to be up Matt spent much time in the organ gallery of the chapel. He used to forget to come for meals and a nurse would have to fetch him. One day I said to him, 'If you don't come at the right time, I'll give you a cold dinner.' He smiled and said, 'Sister, we must feed the soul as well as the body.' ... Some time after Matt's death I asked Mr McDonnell who was a diabetic and returned to hospital periodically if he thought that Matt Talbot, who was in the bed near him, was an exceptionally holy man. He said he certainly was, that he was always praying, even during the night. Matt used to lead the recitation of the rosary in the ward; when he got heart attacks he had considerable suffering. But he never complained. His clothes were old and worn, but spotlessly clean.

Sister M. Dolores McDermott corroborated all that Sister Veronica had said. She commented on his gentleness, his winning smile and how he accepted whatever food was given to him. His sister, a Mr Watt and another friend brought him eggs and fruit when they visited him, but he handed them to the nun without making any remark. He became very ill and was anointed.

> I sent for his sisters and told them that he was dying and well prepared to go. After receiving the Last Sacraments he seemed to be scarcely breathing, but

Sick, suffering and unemployed

thinking back now, I believe he may have been profoundly recollected. The first day he was allowed up he disappeared and could not be found in the hospital or grounds. I was afraid that he had gone out and had had another attack in the street. At last he was found in a corner of the chapel, praying. When I scolded him he replied with his usual quiet smile, 'Sister, I have thanked you and the nurses and doctors and I thought it only right to thank the Great Healer.' His words made a lasting impression on me.

Sisters who observed him in the chapel never saw him use a prayer-book; he was always in a hidden corner and kneeling quite erect. Matt never asked for any privileges and never discussed religious matters. He never showed that he was anything but a good-natured, quiet, holy old man.

On 27 October 1923 Matt was discharged from hospital. He was still very weak and quite unable to work; for some time he had to visit the hospital dispensary regularly. As a member of the Builders' Labourers' branch of the ITGWU he was entitled to National Health Insurance. One of his workmates told him how to apply for it when he first fell ill in June and collected it for him for twenty-six weeks; his sickness benefit of fifteen shillings a week lasted from 4 June to 26 November. After that he was only entitled to draw a disability benefit of 7s 6d. a week.

His friend, Ralph O'Callaghan, not having had a visit from Matt for almost six months, made enquiries about him, and went to the Mater to visit him in St Lawrence's Ward that autumn. When asked how he was, Matt said, 'Oh, I suffered, I suffered.' When he returned to No. 18 Rutland Street Mr O'Callaghan visited him again, bringing a £3 grant from the St Vincent de Paul Society of which he was a member.

I did pity him. He seemed ill and destitute. He looked down and out. I suggested to him that he should go to the Home for the Aged run by the Little Sisters of the Poor in Kilmainham, but that did not appeal to him. 'I would rather be by myself', he said, 'I'm a bit shy.'

Some Vincent de Paul Brothers' leaflets in his books suggest that the Society helped him at this period when he was very badly off. Mr O'Callaghan and other friends, with great difficulty, made him accept gifts of money. Mrs Laird sent him eggs, but he gave them to other tenants in No. 18. Despite his ill health he managed to walk slowly to Gardiner Street and spent many days in the winter of 1924/25 praying there. Brother Furlong saw him one afternoon and asked him how he was feeling. Matt said 'Just middling, Brother, but sure it's the will of God. I'm tired of being idle and hanging around like this. I think I'll go back to work again.'

His illness and frequent lack of money began to take their toll on him. When he paid the rent for his room he had sixpence a week left to live on. That would possibly have allowed him to live, having long since pared his needs to a minimum, but he could not continue his almsgiving. The Poor Clares of Keady, Father Drumgoole's orphans in New York, the Missions, neighbours out of work, acquaintances down on their luck, could no longer count on him for a helping hand. Fortunately Ralph O'Callaghan, the Vincent de Paul Brothers, the Lairds, Ned Fuller, the Larkins and other friends came from time to time; they would chat and, when leaving, would insist that Matt accept 'a little loan to tide you over, until you are back to form'. Mr O'Callaghan made sure that he had warm clothing and that he did not sell garments to be able to help his various charities. There is conflicting evidence as to when Matt went back to work, but his letter — the only one he is known to have written — makes it clear that he was still idle in December 1924; Father Conneely, Editor of the *Far East*, received the letter in that month. It was terse:

Matt Talbot have done no work for past 18 months.

Sick, suffering and unemployed

> I have Been Sick and Given over by Priest and Doctor. I don't think I will work any more there one Pound from me and ten Shillings from my sisser [sister].

Mrs Fylan had looked after him since his return from hospital; in return he gave her the money gifts friends pressed on him during his illness; the donation to the Columban Fathers' missions from her was another gesture of thanks to her, as were occasional sums that she 'put by for emergencies'.

Time was paying out the last months, weeks, days, hours, to the man climbing life's mountain. The final stretch was to call for stiffer endurance but the climber had trained well: suffering, inactivity, a complete severance from the last strands that bound him awaited him before the end. In 1924 his Father-in-God, Dr Hickey, then Monsignor Hickey and President of Clonliffe College, was transferred as parish priest to Haddington Road. Though he still kept in touch with Matt, and told a new parishioner of the holy old man he had left behind on the north side of the city, things were not the same. The regular Saturday evening confessions in Clonliffe were no more, the visits to Rutland Street were fewer as Monsignor Hickey began to cope with his new responsibilities.

Then in January 1925 the new parish priest of Haddington Road, Matt's *anam-chara*, died suddenly. He heard confessions on Saturday and died the following morning, Sunday 20 January. The news must have stunned Matt; he would have recalled how thirty years earlier he first met the priest to whom, as to no one else in this world, he could unburden himself; he would have remembered with gratitude the talks, the sympathy and kindly understanding he had known. Though the death would have come as a shock to him, he hardly grieved; for, to holy friends, death is a matter for joy, not grief.

Matt knew he might die suddenly himself; Dr Moore had warned him of this and when he told his sister she urged him to carry a piece of paper with his name and address in his pocket. Matt said, 'What do I need my name and address for? Won't God be with me when I die?' The Donnellans, living in the flat beneath, were worried because Matt looked so poorly. One night Frank Donnellan offered to stay up with their neighbour or to have their son John stay up, but Matt would not hear of it. 'Not at all. Why should you or John lose your sleep? Both of you have to go to work. If I'm to die tonight, I'll die tonight. No one can keep me if Our Lord wants me.' Frank reported this to his wife Mary, and added, 'If you saw his bed! It's like a switchback railway!'

By Easter 1925 Matt could not stand the inactivity any longer and decided to go back to work again in Martin's yard. Despite his weakened state he prayed more than ever. Mrs Donnellan, seeing him climbing wearily up to his room, said, 'Matt, you're great, all the praying you do.' He said 'I wonder what Our Lord thinks of me. That's what matters.' A long time before he had copied the lines in the *Imitation of Christ:* 'How much each one is in God's sight, that much he is, and no more, sayeth the humble Saint Francis.'

If he looked out of his attic window he could see, not far away, the grey walls and green fields of Clonliffe, with its memories of the day he took the pledge and of the soul-friend, Dr Hickey, he had found there. But Matt was not a man given to gazing out of windows or to sentimental reminiscences. Through the windows of his soul stretched other, more entrancing vistas, limitless expanses; there was no need for remembrance; the best was yet to be.

Soon after Easter 1925 Mrs Manning, who had visited Matt while he was in hospital, was surprised to see him arrive in Martin's yard; he explained that he had come to see Mr Kelly, one of the principals of the firm, to get his job back or to get a small pension. Paddy Laird's recollection of this is somewhat different. He says that Matt was back earlier and some time that spring all the men in Martin's got a rise

Sick, suffering and unemployed

in pay except two, Matt Talbot and another. Their workmates urged them to go to Mr Kelly and ask why they were not getting the increase in wages; but the other man was not the stuff of which heroes are made and, remembering 1913, the men did not want another strike. So, knowing that Matt could be trusted to speak his mind, they persuaded him to go to the Director. Paddy Laird waited in Matt's hut to hear what happened.

> I asked him how he got on. He said he asked why he hadn't been give the rise the other men got but Mr Kelly said, 'Surely *you* don't call yourself a workman?' 'Then I asked for a little pension, enough to help me to pay the rent of the room, and he said that T. & C. Martin's could not afford to pay pensions to all they employed.' And with that Matt sat down and began to cry. When he got control of himself I asked him was there anything more said. Matt replied, 'He said to me, "You don't smoke and you don't drink; though we cannot give you a pension we can give you back the job you had before you got sick".' So he cheered up but it struck me since that Matt was more ill than anyone thought. He came back the next day and everyone welcomed him. When he got his first week's wages he got Masses offered in thanksgiving for being taken back.

Mr Kelly's refusal of a pension did not mean that Martin's was a firm unjust to its workers. Unskilled workers hardly ever got pensions. As a matter of fact Martin's had a high reputation as employers. In 1899, a letter from the Manager of the Port & Docks to the Board on the question of wages, stressed that they (the P & D) were paying labourers two shillings more than the Distilleries Company and 'T. & C. Martin, who handle more timber than any firm in the Port, not only pay their men our rate, 18 shillings per week, for ordinary timber work, but also sixpence per day for piling deals.' The late C.S. Andrews, in his autobiography, *Dublin Made Me*, mentioned that an uncle of his was a timekeeper at Martin's for thirty years without missing one day or being sick all that time. 'The Martins were different from the usual run of employers of their time. They took a personal interest in their employees; when eventually my uncle fell ill and was unable to work for two years before he died, they continued to pay his wages.'

The day after his talk with Mr Kelly, Matt turned up for work at ten minutes to eight, punctual as ever. He did not know that after he left the previous day, the men who worked in his section went in a body to Mr Kelly's office and made it clear that they wanted Matt Talbot kept on in his job for the rest of his days; and, if he had to retire, they expected he would be given a pension in view of his long service and record as a worker. Mr Carew, the foreman, gave Matt a warm welcome. He thought him 'tired and wishy-washy looking', and warned him to take things easy. He also told men working in Matt's area to lend him a hand whenever they could do so quietly and not to let him carry too many planks.

He need not have worried. Ted Fuller, Paddy Laird and Christy Coyle, who now had a second job as warden at Findlater's church, were all more than ready to lighten Matt's work.

> For the timber was heavy. Deals from Canada, ten or twelve feet long, two inches thick and nine inches wide. Matt always kept a pad on his shoulders, partly because the tar from the creosoted deals might drip on his clothes and partly because of his sloping shoulders — without the pad the planks would have slipped off.

By 1925 Ireland, though still suffering from the after-effects of the Civil War, was a different country from that of the preceding decades. Green pillar-boxes and post vans had replaced the red. Khaki uniforms were no longer to be seen on the streets. The Black and Tans were but a nightmare memory. Instead of the black jackets of the 'peelers', the Civic Guards in their navy-blue uniforms were now a familiar sight. Though the fratricidal conflict of 1923-24 had left wounds that would not heal for half a century, there was a climate of lightheartedness, of freedom. Yet, when *A Nation Once Again* was played at public functions or sung at friendly gatherings, many a thought went northward, to the Fourth Green Field, still a province under alien rule.

From the day he returned to Martin's until his death Matt Talbot was never absent from work. More than forty years stood between the Matt of 1884 and the ageing man, now in his seventieth year, of 1925. During those years he had passed for a labouring man, dependable beyond the ordinary, careful and conscientious but silent and self-effacing. A privileged few knew him to be a man of constant prayer and bodily self-denial; fewer still knew of his nightly vigils, his brief repose on plank bed and wooden pillow. Only his confessor and director knew of God's dealings with the little working-man and of that interior life, *hidden with Christ in God.*

His efforts to induce others to adopt spiritual practices he himself had found helpful were not very successful. Only John Gunning was enthusiastic enough to wear a little chain as a badge of servitude to Mary. To a friend who remarked on Matt's unremitting perseverance, he said, 'It's constancy God wants.'

10

Matt reaches his summit

The heatwave that had parched Europe and America in May 1925 reached Dublin a little later. Whit Sunday (31 May), and the Bank Holiday (1 June), were exceptionally cold, with showers of hail and rain; but by mid-week the city sweltered under a broiling sun. The barometer soared and Trinity Sunday, 7 June, dawned in a haze of heat. The hospitals were kept busy and ambulances were in constant demand.

On that Sunday, which he always kept as a special feast, Matt Talbot was out early intent on completing his programme of prayers and Masses. The previous month he had entered his seventieth year. Age was beginning to tell on him. In obedience to Dr Moore he had made slight modifications in his Sunday timetable; it was no longer a question of attending as many Masses as possible; much though he would have liked to, he refrained, knowing that in God's sight obedience ranked higher than sacrifice. In former days he would be at Masses in different churches from early morning, fasting all the time, and ending with 1.00 Mass at the Pro-Cathedral, mother-church of the Archdiocese, St Mary's of the Immaculate Conception, where he had been baptised.

On that morning in 1925 did his mind go back to other red-letter Sundays he had marked in his well-worn bibles and prayer-books? One wonders what happened on a certain Sunday in 1896 when he was moved to write in the margin: 'Lord, thou hast been our refuge always'; or on the Sunday during the 1910 Sacred Heart Novena in Gardiner Street when he wrote: '12th Station, the Crucifixion'; '13th, The Taking Down from the *Cross*'. The Way of the Cross was a favourite devotion of his. When a friend told him how he had seen a priest in Mount Argus going from station to station on his knees, Matt said, 'I would like to do that, but it would be drawing too much attention.' His usual practice was to kneel at each station but to walk from one station to the next.

There is no reason to suppose that he received any forewarning that the Trinity Sunday of 1925 was to be a day of days for him. Even if he had had a premonition he would not have made any change in the Sunday routine he had followed since his illness. To him it was not routine, but the re-enactment and renewal of Calvary as Mass succeeded Mass. For him his union with Christ in the Eucharistic sacrifice and sacrament was a fountainhead of unfailing joy and peace.

His fellow-tenants in No. 18 Rutland Street did not hear him going out that morning, but they were so used to him that they hardly ever noticed him going or coming. People whose work had them afoot early on Sundays, milkmen, Gardaí, paper-sellers, had become so accustomed to seeing his bowed figure outside St Francis Xavier's that afterwards they could not remember whether they had seen him there or not on that particular Sunday. To them he was as familiar a sight as the four columns that front the spacious church at the top of Gardiner Street — the long arterial thoroughfare climbing from where the Custom House skirts the Liffey to the northern rim of the city centre.

The first Sunday of each month was a Sunday when the men's sodality in Gardiner Street had their monthly Mass; Matt and Paddy Laird were always together in the same pew and Paddy remembered that Sunday of 7 June well:

> When after the Mass we stood up and sang a hymn to Our Lady Matt stood and sang with the rest; but when the hymn ended and all knelt Matt forgot to kneel and remained standing, seemingly not taking notice of anything or anyone, until the man on his other side nudged him. It was most unusual for him not to kneel when everyone else did. He paid his usual

monthly subscription; we all paid twopence but Matt always paid a shilling.

Matt must have been in the church from 6.00 a.m. or earlier. Mr Mulvanny, a fellow-tenant in Rutland Street, met him in the hallway there sometime before 9.00 a.m. It was another scorching day. Thinking that Matt looked poorly and remembering that he had spent two month-long periods in hospital the previous year, he advised him to rest. Matt admitted that he felt a bit weak. As the previous Wednesday, Friday and Saturday had been Ember Days, he would have kept the fast then obligatory. He went up to his room and, again remembering the doctor's injunction, took something, probably the cold-tea-and-cocoa mixture that was his only beverage. In a little while he was out again and passed Mulvanny, still in the hall:

> He looked so weak that I suggested he should not go out without resting longer. He smiled, said he felt 'all right and was going to Dominick Street church'. I waited until he went round the corner.... That was the last I saw of Matt alive. I was going to follow him but, knowing that he was a man who did not wish anyone to 'pass remarks' on him, I went to Mass in Gardiner Street instead.

Though the morning was very warm, Matt hurried so as to be in time for the 10.00 Mass in St Saviour's, the Dominican church. Pat Farrell, who had known him for thirty years, said 'He could never get enough of the holy Mass. You'd meet him running to it.' To get to Dominick Street he had to go through Great Charles Street and traverse two sides of Mountjoy Square. A long street, including Gardiner Place, North Great Denmark Street and Gardiner's Row, ended at Parnell Square and the tall spire of 'Findlater's', the Abbey Presbyterian church. Having crossed the main north-south centre-city roadway he hastened his steps along Parnell Square north and into Granby Lane.

Matt reaches his summit

As he turned into the laneway, a short-cut to the church, he ran a few steps, stumbled and collapsed. A visitor from Rugby, a Mr O'Brien, was coming behind Matt:

> He was walking less than five feet in front of me, I saw him shudder, partly turn and fall to the ground. I ran to him as also did a young man named Walsh. We loosened his shirt-collar but I knew he was dead. I ran to Dominick Street Priory and brought a priest. When the priest saw him he knew that life had left him. We knelt down and prayed for the repose of his soul.

Others emerging from the 9.00 Mass or coming for the next Mass joined O'Brien and Walsh and carried Matt from where he fell at the right-hand side of the lane to the doorway of Mrs Keogh's shop at the opposite side. A chemist from Drumcondra and two trainee nurses, a local publican and the usual quota of curious small boys — including the chemist's eight-year old son — were on the scene. One nurse remembered that Dr Eustace was in the church and asked someone to call him; several ran for the priest, Father Reginald Walsh, OP. Mrs Keogh and her son, Myler, fetched a chair, saw the nurse feel his pulse, heard the chemist tell the crowd to stand back and give the man air while he rendered first aid. Two boys, more knowing than their friends, ran to Parnell Square to fetch Garda O'Hanlon who was on duty there. Dr Eustace came, examined the unknown man and pronounced him dead. Later he wrote the following statement:

> I, Dr E.P. Eustace, attended Matthew Talbot on 7 June, 1925 when he died in Granby Lane on his way to the Dominican Priory church. He died on the left side of the road about three feet from the path on the way from Parnell Square. In my opinion he died from heart failure.

Conspicuous in the hushed lane was the tall figure of the Dominican Father, bowed over the still figure that was the cause of all the commotion; draped upon the dust of the laneway, the cream and black of the Dominican's habit looked like a flag — dipped in salute to death.

Garda O'Hanlon phoned for an ambulance and then proceeded to Granby Lane. He interrogated the bystanders but no one knew who the dead man was. Failing to get any particulars as to the identity of the deceased the Garda took some notes:

> Description: about 50 years, 5 feet 8 inches, medium build, brown hair turning grey, nearly bald, grey moustache. He was wearing an old grey tweed suit, 'Kildare House' on tab, black hard hat, black laced boots, blue shirt with red and white stripes.

Although Matt was nearing seventy, the Garda took him to be 'about 50 years'. Men who knew Matt did not agree that he was as tall as the report stated. 'Hardly five feet tall', Martin's men said, while Ralph O'Callaghan described him as 'below middle height'. The suit was one Mr O'Callaghan had given Matt some time previously. When the Corporation ambulance arrived the body was removed to the mortuary in Jervis Street Hospital.

Laurence Thornton, a porter, and Charles Manners, a mortuary attendant, received the body; the House Surgeon pronounced life extinct. A Pro-Cathedral priest, Father McArdle, was sent for. Sister Ignatius, in charge of the accident ward, stated that he came but she did not think he anointed the dead man as they had been informed that he had already been anointed by a Dominican Father in Granby Lane. When the priest left, Mr Manners and the porter undressed the corpse. They found a cord on one arm, a small chain on the other:

> I was cutting his clothing with a scissors when I found a larger chain, with links about half-an-inch long, the

size of a horse's trace, wound round the body. There was also a chain below the knee, so placed that it must have caused him great mortification when kneeling; he had a cord below the other knee. We sent for Sister Ignatius and showed her the chains.

The three witnesses' evidence, given several years later, is somewhat confusing. One described the chains as rusted, another as bright. One thought they had been worn for years; the porter said they were not embedded in the flesh, but that they had worn grooves in the skin which was slightly reddened. Incidentally, a leading present-day Dublin consultant attributes the reddening of the skin, in such hot weather, to the friction of the metal; he says that this could happen if the body-chain were worn for a day or even less. Regarding the grooves, tight clothing, e.g. tops of socks or garters, would easily cause grooves in heatwave temperatures: the chain would do likewise. The nun ordered that the chains be kept aside and put into the coffin later. She thought the dead man looked very ill-nourished, while the two men thought otherwise. Mr Manners felt sure he was an eccentric; Laurence Thornton said 'He's probably a patient escaped from some mental home.' All three commented on how spotlessly clean the deceased was, despite his old and shabby clothes.

More sensation was caused by the discovery of Matt's chains than by any aspect of his life. The assertion of the two men who found them, that he must have worn them for years, conflicted with other statements. Dr Moore, the nursing staff and patients who had seen Matt in the Mater when he was hospitalised in 1923, saw no chains or marks of chains. He went back for check-ups later and still no one saw chains. The book in which Matt read about the chains, *True Devotion to the Blessed Virgin*, was given to him by Ralph O'Callaghan sometime between 1915 and 1924. It was a translation by Father Faber of the Oratory of a work by the Frenchman, Grignion de Montfort, now a canonised saint.

One external practice of the devotion, suggested but not seen as essential, was the wearing of a small iron chain.

Those who adopt this practice, after having shaken off the shameful chains of sin that made them slaves of Satan, and voluntarily surrendered themselves to the glorious slavery of Jesus, are to be praised. With St Paul they glory at being in chains for Jesus' sake.

According to John Gunning, when he and Matt were enrolled at Clonliffe College, they had 'little iron chains, like the chains in a clock'. They were not the only people in Ireland enrolled in the *True Devotion* during the 1920s and 1930s. The late Frank Duff, founder of the Legion of Mary, recommended it strongly to the Legionaries. Moreover, missionary orders preparing novices for the rigours of life in primitive mission fields, also encouraged the wearing of the small chain. However, the terms *slave* and *slavery* were off-putting to many Irish people, just then beginning to savour freedom from the bondage of foreign rule.

Matt had no regular confessor from Dr Hickey's death in January 1925 until his own death six months later. Though occasionally seen at Father Tom Murphy's confessional in Gardiner Street, he lacked the constant spiritual guidance that had been his for thirty years. Though he obeyed Dr Moore's injunctions in regard to diet, he would have tried to compensate by adopting some extra, but different, penance. During the first five months of 1925 Matt Talbot was a sick old man, but an old man intent on doing more and more for God; the only way he could think of doing this was by wearing bigger and heavier chains.

The men in Martin's yards were astounded when they heard of the chains found on his dead body; they declared that he could not possibly have done the heavy work he did while wearing chains, 'and Matt would do as much in one hour as others in two', one said, 'besides, some of us would have noticed it sometime'. This, combined with the

Matt reaches his summit

Mater evidence for 1923, suggests that he did not wear them constantly. His devotion to Our Lady would have prompted him to wear them on Saturdays, her special day; while Sunday, the Lord's Day, was a day when he always practised extra penance. The last word on the chains must be left to his friends and neighbours: 'Matt would have been forgotten the day he died only for the chains: and God gave him the kind of death he got to show the world the sort of man Matt Talbot was.'

Meanwhile no one in Jervis Street had any idea of the dead man's identity. The *Irish Independent* of 8 June carried a paragraph:

UNKNOWN MAN'S DEATH

> An elderly man collapsed in Granby Lane yesterday, and on being taken to Jervis Street Hospital he was found to be dead. He was wearing a tweed suit, but there was nothing to indicate who he was.

On the Sunday night Mrs Fylan came to Rutland Street to tell Frank Donnellan that Matt was missing. He took her to Fitzgibbon Street Garda Station where some enquiries were made by phone but with no result. This was strange, as the Occurrence Book had a report entered that morning by Station Sergeant Tim Maher to the effect that while Garda O'Hanlon was on duty at Parnell Square some boys informed him that an old man was lying unconscious in Granby Lane. The Garda rang for an ambulance, went to Granby Lane and from there to Jervis Street Hospital where the intern, Dr Hannigan, had pronounced the man dead.

Late on Monday night, the Gardaí called on Mrs Fylan and asked her to go to the hospital; she called on Mr Donnellan who accompanied her again. They saw Matt's body and the chains. A nun asked Mrs Fylan 'What are these chains?' Mrs Fylan said that her brother wore them and that they were to be put in the coffin with him. But, before leaving, she took one chain and later gave pieces of it to Mrs Donnellan, Mrs Laird, Martha Doyle, a cousin of the Talbots, and others. In the records of the Processes, i.e. the enquiries made in 1931 and from 1948 to 1953 into Matt's life, Mrs Fylan is described as 'excitable and irrelevant; not a very reliable witness'.

Though Sister Ignatius stated that there was no inquest on Matt, she was mistaken. Dr Louis Byrne, the City Coroner, held an inquest early in the week. The death certificate states that there was an inquest, the cause of death being given as myocardial degeneration. The Dublin Cemeteries Committee's records likewise state: 'Burial on Coroner's Order'. Charles Manners, the mortuary attendant, stated that there was a lot of talk and curiosity in the hospital when news of the chains got around, but that when they were coffining the dead man, one chain was missing. 'People from Rutland Street area came and said that he was a holy man who was once a sinner; I didn't mind them. I was a bit of a cynic.' The missing chain was the one Mrs Fylan had taken; though she had in Matt's lifetime mentioned his fasts and plank bed and nights spent in prayer to various people, she had never mentioned that he wore chains until questioned by the Sister in the mortuary.

Although he died on Sunday 7 June, Matt Talbot was not buried until the following Thursday, the feast of Corpus Christi. On the Wednesday Ralph O'Callaghan learned, quite by accident, of his friend's death and at once took responsibility for the funeral expenses. He also sent word to Father Flood in the Pro-Cathedral, who had previously been in St Laurence O'Toole's and who knew Matt to see and by reputation. John Robins, Ted Fuller and Paddy Laird helped to carry the coffin into Gardiner Street church. Few were present when the coffin was placed in the Sacred Heart chapel; there, on the vigil of the feast of the Blessed Sacrament, the dead man lay where the living man had so often worshipped.

Thursday 11 June was a Church holiday and Matt's funeral took place after 11.00 Mass. Besides the Fylan and Andrews families and some neighbours from Rutland Street there were men from T. & C. Martin's and members of Matt's sodality. Father Flood and Mr O'Callaghan were also present. Dublin being a most sociable city there were many spectators. Already people were speaking of Matt Talbot; his austerities, so long a secret shared with God alone, were no longer unknown. For over forty years he had hidden what he called his 'way of life'. The suddenness of his end revealed what he would have concealed had he got warning of death's approach.

The funeral went out the route so many Dublin funerals take, by the north-west road to Glasnevin Cemetery. The burial ground is on the site of the victory won by the first English invader, Richard FitzGilbert, Earl of Pembroke, Strongbow, over King Roderick O'Connor's army. Since the cemetery had been blessed by Dr Yore in 1832 many a memorable cortège had wended its way to Glasnevin. Philpot Curran was buried there, and O'Connell the Liberator and Mangan the poet. There lies Anne Devlin, so loyal to Emmet, and Hogan the gifted sculptor and scholars like O'Curry and O'Donovan; clergy and laity and, surpassing all in their endurance, generosity and greatness of soul, multitudes of the Dublin poor.

The funeral was a very ordinary one: an elm coffin, a hearse and four white-plumed horses, a mourning coach and two carriages. The cost, including the removal of the remains from Jervis Street Hospital, was £10. The grave was No. SK 319½ in St Bridget's section of the cemetery. Six years later Father Murphy and the men of Matt's sodality in Gardiner Street purchased the adjoining grave space, SK 320, and asked the Cemeteries Committee not to allow any further burial in the two-grave plot. Permission was granted and the sodality given control of the plot.

Matt Talbot's life story became so well known that in 1931 an inquiry was inaugurated by the then Archbishop, Dr

Byrne. Its first session was held on the feast of All the Saints of Ireland, 6 November. This was the first step of the strict procedure followed before any holy person is beatified and allowed to be honoured in any one diocese, country or religious order. If, eventually, the beatus is canonised, the veneration is extended to the entire Church. When the Informative, or diocesan enquiry, ended a carefully collated and authenticated copy of the witnesses' sworn evidence was forwarded to the Holy See. Similarly, at the end of the Apostolic Process or inquiry in 1953, when a greater number of witnesses was interrogated, the evidence was sent to Rome. A papal decree introducing Matt's Cause was signed in 1937.

Canon law regulations for Causes requires that such evidence must be presented in longhand. A team of Dominican nuns was given the task of transcribing the accumulated evidence. The traditional illuminative style of ancient Irish manuscripts was supplied by an artistically gifted Dominican Sister. She must have been drained of energy when she completed the 1,400 pages which were then bound in four volumes and sent on to Rome.

In 1952 Matt Talbot's remains were exhumed and removed to a vault in the central circle of the cemetery, near the tomb of Hogan the sculptor. Distinguished ecclesiastics and lay people were present, including the President of Ireland, Seán T. Ó Ceallaigh who, as an altar-boy, had known Matt and had often seen him praying in Berkeley Road church. When the remains were identified they were transferred to a double coffin, the outer oaken coffin having a brass plate affixed with the inscription:

THE SERVANT OF GOD

MATTHEW TALBOT

The same inscription was on a marble plaque placed over the iron gate of the vault, the coffin being visible through

Matt reaches his summit

the railing of the gate. To that grave, from 1952 to 1972, pilgrims from far and near came to pray. The unemployed of the city trudged to Glasnevin asking Matt to find them work. Missionaries leaving for distant mission fields came to ask the man who so generously helped their work in his lifetime to continue to aid them. Returned exiles and foreign tourists also found their way to Matt's grave.

Standing and praying there one day among the gathering was an illustrious pilgrim, the future Pope Paul VI. Then Cardinal Montini, he was staying with President de Valera at Áras an Uachtaráin; preferring to remain incognito, he cycled from the Park to Glasnevin and, dressed as a priest, paid his respects to one whose life story he had read and in whose Cause he was deeply interested.

No other tomb in that place of noble monuments attracted so many visitors. More than one poet found inspiration there, among them Liam Brophy who penned these lines:

> Although no pomp attend him,
>   The stream's procession all day long
>   Files past him, and the stately throng
> Of surpliced clouds, from rim to rim
>   Of heaven, pass him, and the song
> Of seabirds, where dim islands loom,
> Makes requiem above his tomb.
>
> And though no canopy was spread
>   Above his wrinkled corpse, each night
>   A swift angelic acolyte
> Enkindles stars above his head;
>   And reverentially and light
> The cool asperges of the rain
> Fall on that form, once hot with pain.

Epilogue

Twenty years later, in 1972, the remains were again removed, this time to a church in the heart of the city, Our Lady of Lourdes in Sean MacDermott Street, in the area where Matt spent his life. The tomb of Wicklow granite has a glass panel in front, through which the coffin may be seen. Day in, day out, people come to pray at that tomb, some in ones and twos, others in organised pilgrimages hundreds strong, from overseas as well as from all parts of Ireland. They pray to Matt, asking him to intercede for them; and they pray *for* him, that he may soon be raised to the altars of the Church and given the titles of Blessed and Saint.

Saints are saints, however, not because of the official proclamation, but because they are holy. God, not the proclamation, makes the saint. The secret of Matt's attraction is his holiness, for sanctity has a magnetism all its own. It is indeed something to ponder and wonder at, that a poor man, almost unknown in life, should become famous in death and acquire an influence which extends far beyond the boundaries of Dublin, indeed beyond the shores of his native land. On the building sites a century ago, foremen put Matt first on the line of hod-men 'to set the pace'. It has pleased God, the Master-Builder, in the building of that city not made with hands, to raise up Matt Talbot — *pauper, servus et humilis*, poor, serving and lowly — and put him before us, to set the pace.

Appendix 1

Books read by Matt Talbot in the decade after his conversion (1884-1894):

Several copies of the Bible; separate copies of the New Testament and one copy of St John's Gospel.

The Principles of a Christian Life by Cardinal Bona
The Franciscan Manual for 1884
The Book of Spiritual Instruction by Blosius
The Practice of Christian and Religious Perfection by an unnamed Jesuit
St Augustine's Confessions (10 small volumes)
A Practical Catechism (1770)
Life of St Augustine by Moriarty
The Sinner's Guide
Sanctity and Duties of the Monastic State by Armand de Rance
Directory for Novices of Every Religious Order
On the Sufferings of Our Lord Jesus Christ by Fr Thomas of Jesus, OSA
A History of the Church of Christ
Martyrs of the Coliseum
Life of St Catherine of Siena by her confessor
Life of St Francis Xavier
Lives of the Saints by Butler
Spiritual Conferences by Father Faber
Lives of the Early Christian Martyrs
Lives of Three Oratorians
Life of St Francis de Sales
Virgin Saints of the Benedictine Order
St Paul and his Missions by the Abbé Fouard
Leaves from St Augustine
Writings of St Alphonsus Liguori
The Glories of Mary by St Alphonsus Liguori
The Innocence and Penance of St Aloysius

Remembering Matt Talbot

Treatise on Poverty
Short Treatises on Prayer
Prayer by St Teresa of Avila
Our Lord's Words to Saint Gertrude

(The last twelve books on this list are smaller books and pamphlets.)

Appendix II

Books read by Matt Talbot in the period when he was under Dr Hickey's direction (1895 to 1905 and later):

Manual of Devotion to the Holy Ghost
Life of St Teresa of Avila
Imitation of the Sacred Heart (four volumes) by Father Arnold, SJ
Our Divine Saviour and Other Discourses by Dr Hedley
Meditations on the Life of Our Lord by Father Nouet, SJ
To Obtain Grace to be Preserved from a Sudden and Unprovided Death
Explanation of the Ceremonies of Holy Week
The Blessed Sacrament, Centre of Immutable Truth by Cardinal Manning
The Shield of the Catholic Faith by Tertullian
St Catherine of Genoa on Purgatory
The Imitation of Christ
The Spiritual Combat
Introduction to a Devout Life by St Francis de Sales
The Mass
Lives of the Irish Saints
Life of St Bridget of Sweden
Life of St Rita of Cascia
Life of St Gerard Majella
Life of St Catherine of Siena
Life of St Augustine
Our Lord's Revelations to St Gertrude
On Reading (reprint of a lecture) by Dr Hedley
All for Jesus by Father Faber
Lives of Eminent Saints of the Oriental Deserts
History of the French Clergy During the Revolution by the Abbé Barruel

He also had several anti-proselytising pamphlets of the period and leaflets with litanies to the Blessed Trinity, Our

Lord, Our Lady and ten saints, including our own St Dympna; some leaflets with prayers and litanies for a happy death.

Appendix III

Books lent to Matt Talbot by Ralph O'Callaghan between 1914 and 1924 approximately:

Christian Perfection by Rodriguez
Butler's Lives of the Saints, (twelve volumes)
Growth in Holiness by Father Faber
Creator and Creatures by Father Faber
The Blessed Sacrament by Father Faber
Watches of the Passion by Father Galwey, SJ
The Catholic Doctrine of Grace by Joyce
Digest of the Doctrine of the Incarnation by St Thomas Aquinas
Holy Communion by Dalgairns
The Temporal Mission of the Holy Ghost by Cardinal Manning
England and the Sacred Heart by Price
Ortus Christi by Mother St Paul
Catholic Mysticism by Algar Thorold
Meditations on the Mysteries of the Holy Rosary by Père Monsabre, OP
Catechism, Doctrinal, Moral etc. by Power
Christian Inheritance by Dr Hedley
Catechism of the Council of Trent
Modern Infidelity Exposed by Robertson
True Devotion to Mary by B. Grignion de Montfort
Miniature Lives of the Saints (two volumes) by Bowden
Anima Devota by Father Pagini
Reeve's History of the Bible
Large Life of St Vincent de Paul by Bougard
Life of Thomas à Kempis by Cruise
Life of Cardinal Franzelin by Fr Walsh, SJ
Study of Lost and Saved by Father Walsh, SJ
Life of St Patrick by Father Morris
Franciscan Tertiaries by Father William
Life of St Elizabeth of Hungary
Life of Mother Marie de Jésus
Life of St Magdalen de Pazzi by Father Farrington, OCC

Remembering Matt Talbot

Life of Father Faber by Bowden
Life of Pius IX by Maguire
Life of St Laurence O'Toole
The Present Position of Catholics by Cardinal Newman
Life of Cardinal Manning
The Ancient Irish Church by Father Gaffney
Mariae Corona by Sheehan
Ways of God, Story of a Conversion
The Pope and the People
St Catherine of Siena (two-volume Life) by Drane

Appendix IV

Other books owned by Matt Talbot and now with those listed in Appendices I and II and kept in 'Matt Talbot's Box' in Archbishop' House, Dublin, include:

Meditations on the Love of God by Père Grou
Elevation of the Soul to God by R. Staples, OCD
The Crucifix, the Most Wonderful Book in the World by Fr McLoughlin
Cost Thought in Time by Monsignor Ward
Essays on Miracles by Cardinal Newman
Christ among Men by Père Sertillanges
The Providence of God: A Sacred Heart Novena by Fr J Murphy, SJ
The Science of the Soul
St Leo the Great and the Dogma of the Incarnation by the Bishop of Leeds
Life of Suarez
Life of Cardinal Newman
Life of Père Lacordaire
Life of Cardinal Bellarmine by Aubrey Gwynn, SJ
Life of St Teresa by Robert Kane, SJ
Life of Venerable Oliver Plunkett
Life of St Philip Neri
Life of St Vincent Ferrer
Life of St Margaret Mary
Life of Blessed Thomas More
Addresses of the late Fr T Burke, OP
Addresses on the Evils of Drunkenness by Father R. Kane, SJ
Discourses on the Perfections and Wonderful Works of God
Religion of the Hebrew Bible by Hitchcock
The Church in Scotland by H.G. Graham
Palm Sunday by H Thurston, SJ
Book, Bell and Candle: Exorcism and Anathema by H. Thurston, SJ
Christian Science by H. Thurston, SJ

Powers and Origin of the Soul by P.M. Northcote
The Church in Portugal by C. Torrend, SJ
Some Facts about Martin Luther by Attenridge
The Oath against Modernism by S.M. Smith, SJ
Jesuit Obedience by S.M. Smith, SJ
'Secret Instructions' of the Jesuits by J. Gerard, SJ
What the World owes to the Papacy by Monsignor Grosch

Most of the works in this last section were acquired between 1915 and 1925.

The Intellectual Claims of the Catholic Church by B. Windle
Will any Religion Do? by an unnamed Benedictine writer
Life of St Colmcille
Life of St Columbanus by Dr Myles Ronan
The Plot, German or English? by 'Lector'
The Case against the Promised Boundary Commission by 'Lector'
The Nationalist Case Stated
Catholicism and Peace
The Pope in Peace and War
Memoirs of an Exiled Priest of '98
What is Orangeism?
Between Capitalism and Socialism by Dr Coffey
A Living Wage and a Family Wage by Dr Keane, OP
The Social Value of the Gospel by Leon Garriguet
The Church, a Mother to Love and be Proud of by Dr Keane, OP
History of the Roman Empire
History of Peter the Great of Russia
Leo X and the Character of Lucretia Borgia
University Life in the Middle Ages
Loss and Gain by Cardinal Newman
Silence and Recollection by Dr Daniel Murray, Archbishop of Dublin
Apologia pro Vita Sua by Cardinal Newman
The School of Christ by Père Grou
Life of St Ursula
Life of St John the Evangelist

Appendix IV

Life of St Rose of Lima
Life of St John Francis Regis
Life of St Vincent de Paul

Scripta

On pieces of paper inserted in his books Matt Talbot copied the following extracts and made notes on spiritual matters:

— God is the wisdom of a purified soul.
— There is only one step between me and death.
— There is no tomorrow for a Christian.
— Who can understand sins? From my secret ones, cleanse me, O Lord, and from those of others spare thy servant.
— God will not ask us how eloquently we have spoken, but how well we have lived.
— Cleanse me, O Lord, from unknown sins. Deliver me, O Lord.
— That men should make use of God for His own glory is beyond what we can think of.
— To know God and to understand His ways and to watch in His presence in all sanctity is the great end of life.
— Man can fly from everything in nature but he cannot fly from himself.
— As to nobility of blood, true nobility is to be derived only from the blood of the Son of God. God, says St Augustine, can only be honoured by love.
— The obedience of Jesus Christ to the Will of God was the recognition of the Sovereignty of God over the will of men. I ask you, O God, to blot out all my sins in the Name of Our Lord Jesus Christ.
— Jesus Christ is at once the beginning, the way and the immortal end which we must strive to gain, but above all in Holy Communion he is the Life of our souls.
— Let us not forget that Jesus wished to be cursed on the Cross that we might be blessed in the Kingdom of His Father.
— As I cannot receive Thee, my Jesus, in Holy Communion, come spiritually into my heart and make it Thine forever.
— The Son of God by becoming man sanctified all the states

Scripta

and conditions of men. Jesus was not always preaching or healing but he always prayed and suffered.
— Oh, Jesus, mortify within me all that is bad; make it die. Put to death in me all that is vicious and unruly. Kill whatever displeases Thee, mortify in me all that is my own. Give me true humility, true patience and true charity. Grant me the perfect control of my tongue.
— How I long for You to be master of my heart, my Lord Jesus.
— Jesus, says Origen, is the Sun of Justice, arising with the Spring of grace upon our hearts.
— The Heart of Jesus is with me. Stop. Cease. The people of Antioch, it is related, once arrested a violent earthquake by writing on the doors of their Houses. Jesus is with us. Cease.
— What think ye of Christ? (This was written on the back of a picture of Christ teaching in the temple, used as a book-marker by Matt.)
— Grant me, O Jesus, Thy Grace and love and I shall be rich enough.
— The sparrow hath found herself a house and the turtle dove a nest for her young. Thy Heart, O Jesus, shall be my rest and repose.
— May my eyes and my heart be always on the wound of Thy Blessed Heart, O Jesus.
— Who shall separate us from the love of Jesus?
— Heart of Jesus, be Thou the object of all the affections of my heart.
— Lord, give me of that water flowing from Thy Heart and I shall never thirst.
— Heart of Jesus, support the weak, clothe me with Thy strength.
— Mary, Mother of Jesus, pray for me.
— O Mary, conceived without sin, pray for me who flies to thee.
— Refuge of sinners, mother of those who are in their agony, leave us not in the hour of our death.

- O Blessed Mother, obtain from Jesus a share of His folly.
- O Virgin, I ask only three things: the grace of God, the Presence of God, the Blessing of God.
- The Blessed Virgin Mary is glorified by our devotion to the Angels.
- The Angels merit our love for they will assist us at the hour of death. The Angels help us in temporal things.
- Saint Teresa was once weeping. When asked why she wept she said: For three things — God — Soul — Death.
- St Bernard says: Who shall give water to my eyes now and fountains of tears to my head that I may prevent weeping in hell by weeping now?
- St John speaks of the lust of the flesh, the lust of the eyes and the pride of life. They are nothing else but the love of pleasure, the love of riches and the love of honour.
- St Ambrose says that without combat there is no victory, and without victory there is no crown.

The remainder of the scripta deal not only with the spiritual life, doctrine and devotion but with secular matters. The following examples give a fair idea of the whole:

- Poverty is the foundation of Christian perfection and makes this den of thieves a house of prayer.
- Faith is an act of the will.
- The yc zcar czar (sic) of Russia his income is 20 mill year, his demain (sic) is big as Ireland.
- There are 72 churches in honour of the Blessed Virgin within the walls of Rome.
- At confession you ask for the priest's blessing. He says: May the Lord be in your heart and on your lips that you may truly and humbly confess your sins.
- Denis Lacy shot dead Glen aherliw (sic).
- In the lifetime of St Philip Neri there were 15 Popes.

— The Kingdom of Heaven was promised not to the wise and educated but to such as have the spirit of little children.
— McCulagh's hour is from 3 to 5.
— Mr McCugh's hour is from 2 to 3 and 7 to 8. (This and the last entry suggest that Matt enrolled friends to make a Holy Hour at set times.)
— Charles Talbot, Middle Gardiner Street 16 March 1899 (Father's death).
— The three exterior acts of religion are Adoration, Sacrifice and Vows.
— Obedience to lawful authority is of right divine. In 1832 Gardiner Street church was opened.
— There were 21 German translations of the Bible, 15 in High German, 6 in Low German, before Luther. Luther himself used a translation of St Nicholas of Myra which appeared in 1473.
— Lucius and his wife of Great Britain.
— It is a fact that spirits act upon matter.
— Offer yourself to God with joy and peace. Say one *Our Father* and one *Hail Mary* in honour of Jesus' life of ignominy.

There are many longer extracts; the foregoing suffice to show how carefully Matt Talbot read and noted down what struck him. Some extracts suggest that he had asked to have certain ideas explained, perhaps by his director, and later jotted down the answer. One wonders what led to the inclusion of this final trenchant note:

> Sir Henry Wotton, a great authority on the point, Ambassador at Venice, tells us that an Ambassador is one sent to foreign Courts to invent lies for his country's good.

Bibliography

Primary sources

Official reports/records
Evidence given at the tribunals set up in 1931 and 1948 to enquire into the life of Matt Talbot, Dublin Diocesan Archives
Birth and marriage certificates in the Pro-Cathedral and the churches of St John the Baptist, Clontarf and St Agatha's, North William Street
Roll-books of St Laurence O'Toole's and O'Connell's Christian Brothers' Schools; also Christian Brothers' records for 1937, 1938
Records of the Dublin Port & Docks Board
Records of the ITGWU
Extract from Archbishop Cullen's evidence before the House of Commons Select Committee enquiring into the Poor Law in Ireland, 27 May 1861

Interviews
Notes taken by the author between 1950 and 1953 with approximately fifty people who knew Matt Talbot well, including two who knew him since childhood
Interviews with the late Archbishop McQuaid regarding some evidence given during the tribunals of 1931 and 1948
Interview with the late Dr Myles Ronan, PP
A collection of audio-cassettes with recorded interviews by Father Morgan Costelloe, Vice-Postulator of Matt Talbot's cause, and by makers of documentary films on Matt, with several persons who either knew him or who had relevant information (I am indebted to Father Costelloe for lending me these cassettes.)

Bibliography

Newspapers/journals
Dublin and London newspaper files for 1853, 1885-1887, 1909, 1913, 1914, 1916, 1921, 1923, 1925, 1952

Dublin Journal of Medical Science, May 1845

Reference works
Catholic Directories, 1853-1885
Whitakers, Thoms, Postal and other street directories, 1853-1899

Additional sources
Books, leaflets, papers, scripts, etc., in Matt Talbot's box of books at Archbishop's House, Drumcondra

Secondary sources

	Random Notes of a Reporter, Dublin, 1920
Andrews, C.S.	*Dublin Made Me,* Dublin, 1979
Augustine, Father	*Footprints of Father T. Matthew,* Dublin, 1947
Blosius	*A Book of Spiritual Instruction,* (translated by B.A. Wilberforce), London, 1900
Booth, C.	*Ireland, Industrial and Agricultural,* Dublin, 1901
Chart, G.	*Unskilled Labour in Dublin: Housing and Living Conditions,* Dublin, 1914
A Christian Brother	*A Century of Catholic Education: Brother Burke and his Associates,* Dublin, 1916
Cooke, J.	*Government Enquiry into Dublin Housing Conditions: Evidence of J. Cooke, Secretary NSP,* Dublin, 1913
Daly, M.	*The Deposed Capital,* Cork 1984

Donnelly, N. — *History of the Dublin Parishes*, Dublin, 1905-1911
Fingall, Countess of — *Sixty Years Young: Memoirs*, London, 1932
Fitzpatrick, W.J. — *Father T. Burke, OP*, London, 1885
Fitzpatrick, W.J. — *History of the Dublin Catholic Cemeteries*, Dublin, 1900
Fleetwood, J., MB — *History of Medicine in Ireland*, Dublin, 1951
Gerrard, F. — *Picturesque Dublin, Old and New*, London, 1898
Gibbons, M. — *Life of Margaret Alyward*, London, 1928
Glynn, Sir T. — *Life of Matt Talbot*, Dublin, 1928
Horgan, J.J. — *Parnell to Pearse*, Dublin, 1948
ITGWU — *The Attempt to Smash the ITGWU*, Dublin, 1924
O'Neill, Phil — *Twenty Years of the GAA*, Kilkenny, 1925
Puirséil, Pádraig — *The GAA in its Time*, Dublin, 1982
O'Riordan, M. — *Catholicity and Progress in Ireland*, St Louis, 1906
Rogers, P. — *Father Theobald Matthew*, Dublin, 1943
Ronan, M. — *An Apostle of Catholic Dublin*, Dublin, 1944
Ryan, D. (ed.) — *The Workers' Republic*, Dublin, 1951
Ryan W P. — *The Irish Labour Movement*, Dublin, 1919
Webb, J.J. — *Industrial Dublin since 1698*, London, 1913
Wright, A. — *Disturbed Dublin*, London, 1914